TATTING

A New Look at the Old Art of Making Lace

Books by Lael Morgan

Tatting: A New Look at the Old Art of Making Lace
And the Land Provides
The Woman's Guide to Boating and Cooking

TATTING

A New Look at the Old Art of Making Lace

By Lael Morgan

DOUBLEDAY & COMPANY, INC.
Garden City, New York
1977

Frontis:
"Ludicrous Lion," a picture tatted by the author.

Library of Congress Cataloging in Publication Data
Morgan, Lael.
  Tatting.
  1. Tatting.   I. Title.
TT840.M63   746.4'36

All photographs by the author unless otherwise noted.

ISBN 0-385-07707-6
Library of Congress Catalog Card Number 76–2808

Acknowledgments

To Norma Bowkett, that one in a million. I taught her to tat and she improved upon my method. She also lent her hands, camera, and granddaughter to this project.

To Tykie Malloy whose patient search of the antique and book stores of Maine kept me up on what was old.

And to Elsa van Bergen who suggested speeding up the process.

Preface

When I was nine my mother sent me off to Vermont to visit her mother, Flora May Abbott, who was a fine lady, and Flora May taught me to tat. I wasn't a precocious little girl and subsequent aptitude tests showed I should become a forest ranger, so you'd think I wasn't the tatting type, but I learned quickly and I loved it.

The forest rangers said they would hire me but, because I was female, I could never advance in their ranks, so I said to heck with that and became a writer-photographer and managed to tailor my work to the point where I now spend half of each day outdoors, climbing about the wilds.

But I still tat. I tat when I'm forced to come indoors and visit with people. If I don't tat, I fidget.

I tat on cross-country airplane trips and on Greyhound buses. I used to knit, but on one Los Angeles/Maine trek I mismatched a sweater front and gave the whole thing up as too bulky. Tatting fits in a small, vacant corner of my camera case.

I tatted sailing across the Pacific in a 36-foot schooner. Reading made me seasick.

I tatted in spare moments out whale hunting with the Alaskan Eskimos. (Some day some anthropologist visiting our digs will probably think that the Eskimos invented tatting, what with all the boot and parka trims I turned out.)

I tatted while keeping an eye out for scorpions and coral snakes, camping with the Huichol Indians in the Sierra Madre mountains of Mexico.

And I tatted at Fish and Game Board meetings. I was the first woman ever appointed to the Alaska board, and two of the ol' boys complained to the chairman that it didn't look right for a woman to be sitting there making lace while deliberating on salmon escapment and hunting regulations for antlerless moose, but the chairman said he only wished *he* could tat, and I tatted blissfully on.

There are what I call "empty headed" tatting patterns that don't take much thought. That's for Fish and Game. But—don't let

Chapter II fool you—there are some tatting patterns that take so much concentration you don't hear three-alarm fire warnings—the golden butterfly, page 91, for example. These are useful for those days of "profound sorrow and sadness" notes by the Queen of Romania in Chapter I . . . or for when the weather is inclement.

And tatting is such a pretty thing to do. Thank you for it, Flora May Abbott! And may you, good reader, enjoy the results of her teaching.

Contents

I

A Royal Art Revisited

Tatting—the genteel art of making fine lace with a shuttle—almost got lost in the rush of the twentieth century. In your great-grandmother's day it was the rage. Ladies tatted because they looked so graceful at the work and because they needed beautiful laces to trim their ornate dresses and edge their linens.

Even into the 1950s women's handwork magazines carried tatting designs, but the popularity of the lace died out with the last generation of great-grandmothers. Books on tatting have become rare books. You'll find them listed as such in public libraries, but you'll also find, if you go to read them, that many are missing—stolen.

With the resurgence of interest in handwork —particularly macramé—women and a few bold men are again turning to tatting, but there is little material available to the beginner who doesn't resort to thieving. Most needlework encyclopedias still include a token chapter on the subject, but these are not particularly helpful. One of the most complete

handbooks on the market is candid about it. In the introduction the writer admits, "The technique [of tatting] is somewhat difficult to describe. If you do not know how to tat and would like to learn, try to augment the information in this chapter with a lesson or two from a friend who knows the art." The problem is that friends like that are one in a million.

But tatting is not difficult. There is only one stitch to master—actually two half hitches,

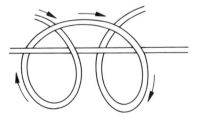

which is a common seaman's knot. The word tatting, itself, comes from the French *tâter,* to touch. "It does not need thought or counting and is ideal to pick up in a moment's leisure," an old book on the subject notes.

Some researchers will tell you that early Egyptians discovered tatting, while others credit the Chinese or the Italians. The idea had, no doubt, been around for centuries, when it came into vogue as a simple and inexpensive means of imitating fine laces. By the 1700s, however, European nobility had taken up the art—and certainly not for thrift.

Charles Sedley, eighteenth-century poet, wrote "The Royal Knotter" as a tribute to the handwork of his English queen who was a tatting buff.

Oh happy people! We must thrive
Wilst thus the Royal Pair do strive
Both to advance your glory
While he (by valour) conquers France
She manufactures does advance
And makes thread fringes for ye!

Three antique and beautifully decorated tatting shuttles. The white celluloid one on the lower left belongs to Susanna Lewis; the engraved silver shuttle and the one embossed with blue forget-me-nots are in the private collection of Helene Von Rosenstiel.

Blessed we! Who from such queens are freed
Whom by vain Superstition led,
Are always telling beads.
For here's a queen now, thanks to God!
Who when she rides in coach abroad
Is always knotting threads.

Sir Joshua Reynolds painted the Countess of Albemarle tatting, and she tatts still in the National Gallery in London. There is a portrait by J. M. Nattier of Madam Adelaide of France with a large tatting shuttle at Versailles. And history recorded that on November 4, 1755, one Lazare Duvaux furnished Madame de Pompadour with a shuttle in gold enameled with ribbons for £690. It is also

Exquisite examples of nineteenth-century Irish tatted lace (courtesy, The Metropolitan Museum of Art, Gift by subscription, 1909, Blackborne Collection).

Tatted doily by Flora Abbott, grandmother and teacher of the author.

known that in January of 1765 the lady lost that shuttle at the Comédie-Française but we don't know whether or not it was returned to her.

During this period tatting was often referred to as "knotting," especially by the English, and indeed, it was not tatting as we know it today. As yet no one had devised a means of joining individual tatted rings, which left the work loosely structured; dependent on being sewed down.

The problem was solved in the mid-1800s, with one Mlle. Eleanore, Riego de la Branchardiere taking credit. Mlle. Riego de la B. was the first to join tatted rings by means of the decorative loops (she called them pearls, we call them picots) that surround them, and her designs were widely purchased in book series. Tatting became even more popular and there were more refinements. Since tatted lace now had body and no longer needed to be sewn together, finer threads could be used and smaller shuttles were developed, often with a pointed pick or hook to facilitate joining.

In this era—the dawn of inexpensive printing and ladies' magazines—new ideas spread fast, and each inventive design quickly inspired another.

The most dedicated tatter was Carman Sylva, Queen of Romania, who, in 1910, wrote the introduction to a magnificent tatting book by Katherin L. Hoare, her lady-in-waiting.

The Queen dedicated the book to women like herself "who afford to stay at home, to have ten or twelve children and be happy in bringing them up to be good and clever and useful.

"Here is pretty work to do while reading—

Our work is for human eternities!
Carmen Sylva
May 1910

Queen of Romania at work with her tatting shuttle; autographed for Lady Hoare's book, The Art of Tatting. *On the right is an example of the Queen's work, a lovely gold and pearl chalice cover (courtesy for both: General Research and Humanities Division, The New York Public Library, Astor, Lenox and Tilden Foundations).*

much prettier than knitting," the Queen maintained. "Nowadays work has become quite a luxury as everything useful and necessary is done by machine. Then let this luxury be as beautiful as we can make it."

The year was 1910, well before women's liberation, and the Queen—who was built like Queen Victoria and thought along the same lines—observed:

Some men don't like it when ladies work [but] —how much care and sorrow, how much deep anxiety, what profound sorrow and sadness is put into silent women's work. One ought always to look at it with awe and reverence, not only on account of the patience it teaches but more for the silently borne pain it has hid. Many a woman can say: "What a blessing that my work cannot speak!"

There is many a tear hidden in women's work, many a sigh breathed into it, many a word repressed that spoken might have done irretrievable harm . . .

Tatting has the charm of lacemaking and weaving combined. It is the same shuttle as in the weaving loom only the loom is our fingers and the shuttle obeys our thoughts and the invention of the movement. The joy when a new stitch is found is very great. I don't know if Madame Curie felt much happier when she found radium . . .

Don't despise our needle and our shuttle, don't think that our thoughts need be small for all that! The mothers of very great men could only knit or spin. The weaving of Penelope has become symbolic.

Woman is most solitary, even in her household, even doing man's work. Only when she is made into the part of the machine does she stop being a woman.

A woman's hand is never so graceful as when working on some lovely piece of art.

The book contains many samples of the Queen's work—including a gold-and-silk iconostasis (church) curtain set with turquoises—showing she was indeed an artist with the shuttle. And, like Madame Curie, she had her share of discoveries. Some of the techniques described in Lady Hoare's book (such as concealing and strengthening knots by working thread ends into stitches) have been

lost over the years, but I find them extremely useful in my work.

Tatting remained popular until World War I. Handbooks of that era show directions for dress tops, bedspreads, tablecloths, antimacassars, and even window-shade pulls. But through the war years, dress became simpler and so did our lifestyle. We cut down on the trimmings.

The French call tatting *frivolité,* which also translates "frivolous or trivial," and so it may seem. One can use only so many fine lace collars, and edged handkerchiefs are reserved nowadays mostly for weddings. Yet tatting is unusually strong and durable. Far more so than ordinary lace or crochet, which unravels easily. It also takes less concentration than many handcrafts and is less awkward to manage on airplanes and in waiting rooms.

Taking these things into consideration— and being a dedicated tatter who enjoys the work—I began finding practical uses for the art. I hate lace-trimmed sheets. Antimacassars won't stay on plastic blow-up chairs or leather

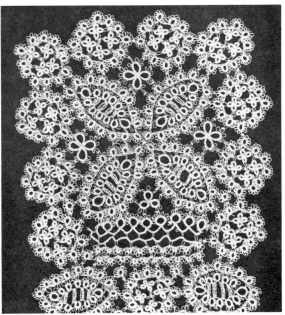

Two American examples of tatting from the late nineteenth century. On the left, a delicately patterned doily; on the right a decorative tie (courtesy of The Brooklyn Museum, Gift of Mrs. Lillian G. Pierce).

couches. And I don't have any window shades that need lace pulls. But I do love feminine clothing, bright wall hangings, and colorful trim.

Traditionally, tatting has been limited to fine threads—mostly whites and pastels—but for no good reason. If the Queen of Romania could tat gold wire, I decided, I could tat dyed hemp.

Dyed hemp, of course, won't fit on the con-ventional tatting shuttle, but that didn't prove a problem. I found I could work it with a Nor-wegian fishnet needle and, later, with a simple shuttle of my own manufacture, which I've modestly named the Morgan Shuttle.

This book—the results of my experimenting—is just the beginning and, hopefully, it will take tatting out of the realm of *frivolité* and give it a useful spot in the modern world.

II

How to Tat

Tatting looks difficult; all that fancy finger-work with threads flying! Well, don't let it dazzle you. Actually *all* there is to tatting is one knot done in two steps—a simple half hitch that even the dumbest Boy Scout could master. Tatting half hitches run free over another thread like the knot of a noose.

Creative tatters arrange these knots in rings, squares, triangles, octagons, crescents, and stars; bridge them with chains; hang them from strings; bracket them with beads; work them into a field of lace; or use them as edging trim. All this—and more if you have the imagination—with just that simple half hitch.

Beginning tatters usually make just one mistake. At a crucial point in forming the basic knot there are two threads that can be pulled, and amateurs are apt to pull the wrong one. The knot forms upside down and won't run free. Jams the works. But this is easy enough to correct if you know what to watch for.

One other problem sometimes encountered is that beginners worry too much about how they hold the shuttle, rather than where they push it. When I started tatting I worried about

that, too, until I discovered there are any number of holds or thrusts that will do the job if you know where you're going. (This applies particularly to left-handed learners. Concentrate on the route of the shuttle rather than hand holds and finger positions.)

The tatting method my grandmother taught me is classic and elegant. In those days my manual dexterity quotient was considered to be zilch (mainly because I refused to learn to tie my shoes), and I thought it brave of Gram to undertake such a task, but later I found that the classic method is the easiest to teach if students don't take it too seriously. All those poised, crooked fingers really open up the work so you can see where the shuttle goes. And once you learn that, you can sluff along with any hand hold that feels comfortable.

The classic method does not go well with the new big shuttle, and so it is best to learn with the small, standard model. Once you master that, use of the larger shuttle will come easily. Because of its length it must be passed through the fingers, but that comes naturally once you understand the route it must take.

CLASSIC TATTING METHOD

Choose a small, traditional shuttle that feels comfortable in your hand. The older design with no movable parts and a pinlike pick in place of a hook is my first choice. Usually there is a hole through the center shaft through which you can anchor thread before winding. If you choose a modern shuttle with a removable bobbin, make sure there is pressure enough on the sides of the shuttle to keep the bobbin from unwinding when you need to pull off more working thread. If the bobbin is cranky, remove it and pinch together or pry apart shuttle sides accordingly.

To wind bobbin, remove it from shuttle and

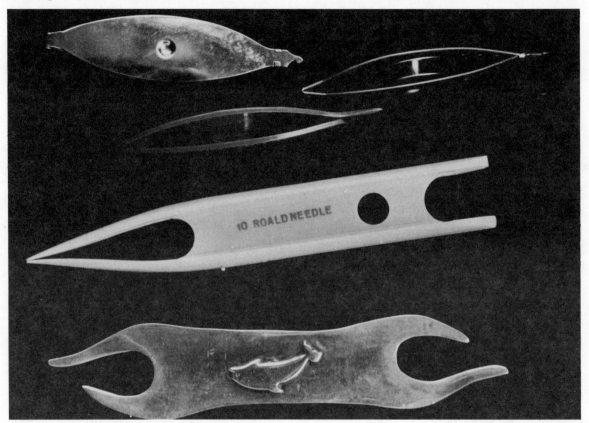

Traditional tatting shuttles (top row) are still a standard item in many variety stores. The metal type has a removable bobbin and crochet hook end. An older design (below) has no movable parts and a pinlike pick in place of the hook. Some prefer it because there is no chance of the bobbin jamming or the hook catching in fine work. In the center is a Norwegian net needle which can be purchased through houses that supply commercial fishing gear. It works well for tatting heavy yarns and hemp but lacks a pick or hook for joining. At the bottom is the Morgan yarn shuttle which I find best for working heavy materials. This one is of sterling silver and has a whale design so I won't feel so bad when I run out of thread, but they need not be so fancy.

hold end of thread with thumb to inside of little spool. Wind thread around bobbin, pulling thread firmly so that it is anchored. When bobbin is wound fat, snap it back into shuttle.

How to Hold Hands

Loop shuttle thread loosely around four fingers on left hand, pinching joint of loop between thumb and index finger. Unwind about 20 inches of thread from shuttle. Hold shuttle loosely between thumb and index finger of right hand, with head pointed toward loop over left hand. Easy does it. A death grip gets you nowhere, makes your hands sweaty and smears the thread. You are now ready to begin the basic knot in tatting.

Basic Knot and Ring

Step 1. The first knot is simply a half hitch around the loop. Once it is loosely formed, relax all fingers of loop hand except thumb and index finger holding the work, and pull firmly on shuttle thread. This will cause loop thread around hand to change position and circle shuttle thread. After loop thread circles shuttle thread, spread loop fingers carefully, bringing the stitch (little knot just made) to rest at loop joint between thumb and index finger.

Note: *It is very important to relax fingers within loop while pulling on shuttle thread or loop thread will knot, fouling work.*

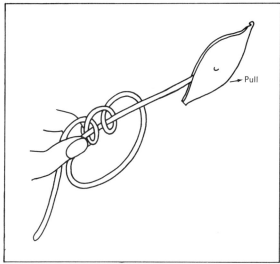

Completing Basic Tatting Knot

Step 2. Change position of shuttle in right hand so that it lies on upturned palm with its head pointed between open fingers of loop hand. Now you make a second half hitch from the other direction. After it forms loosely around the loop thread, relax all fingers on the loop hand except thumb and index finger holding the work. This will cause loop thread around hand to change position and circle shuttle thread. (See Note, Step 1.) When it does, spread loop fingers carefully bringing the stitch (the half-hitch knot just formed) to rest at loop joint beside knot made in Step 1. This completes and locks the basic tatting knot which is referred to as the double stitch (ds).

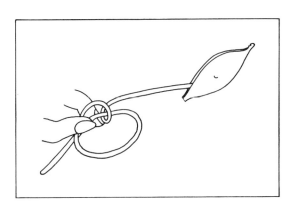

Basic Knot—right way

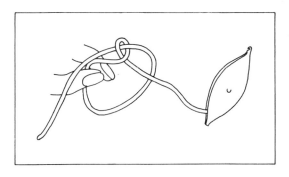

Basic Knot—wrong way

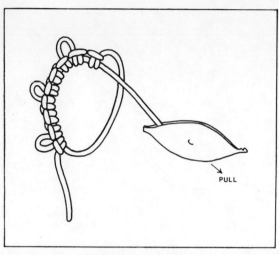

Closing the Ring

Also keep in mind that there are many variations in holding shuttles, and once you understand the direction in which the shuttle must go, you may change finger movements to suit yourself. Usually, I start with the classic method, then lapse into something lazier as my fingers tire or my mood changes. No matter, as long as the tension (tightness or looseness) remains the same.

Josephine Knot

Sometimes to make work spiral only Step 1 of the basic double stitch is used. This is called a Josephine Knot.

When you have made enough double stitches for the size of the ring required, grip the joint of the loop between thumb and index finger of left hand, remove other fingers from loop and pull shuttle thread with right hand until loop closes like a noose. How tight you pull the noose depends on your tatting style. My work is generally tight but working loosely is not wrong; it simply gives the work a fatter look which is particularly attractive when working with heavy yarns.

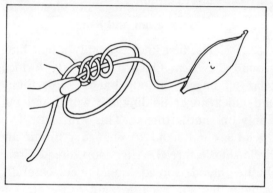

Josephine Knot

Classic Method For Rings, Step by Step
(Photo credit: Norma Bowkett)

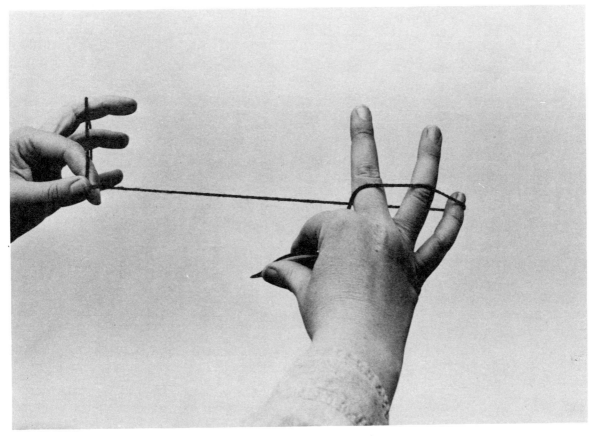

Loop shuttle thread loosely around four outstretched fingers of left hand, pinching joint of loop between thumb and index finger. Hold shuttle loosely in right hand with head between thumb and index finger, pointed toward left hand, with shuttle thread held taut over back of second, third, and little fingers of right hand, then running under them.

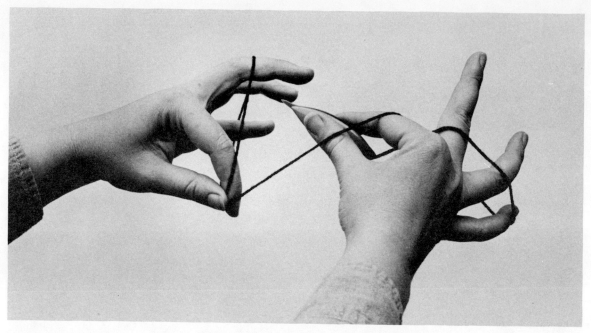

Pass shuttle under its own thread.

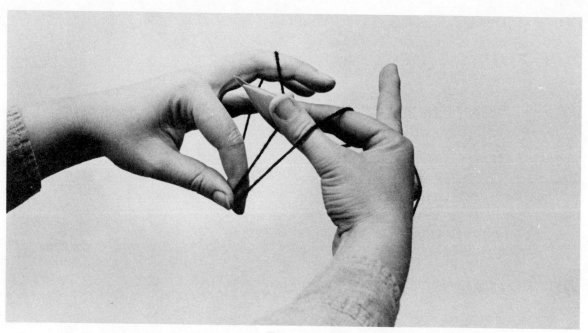

Pass shuttle under loop between index and second finger of left hand with loop thread going over top of shuttle, sliding first index finger holding shuttle and then over tail of shuttle. Pull shuttle back over loop (inside thread that runs over back of right hand) with loop thread passing between thumb and bottom of shuttle.

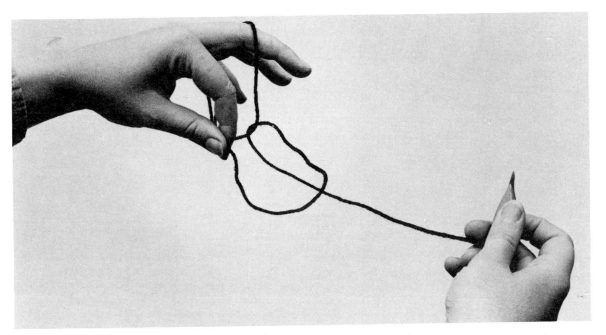

Shuttle thread will circle loop thread.

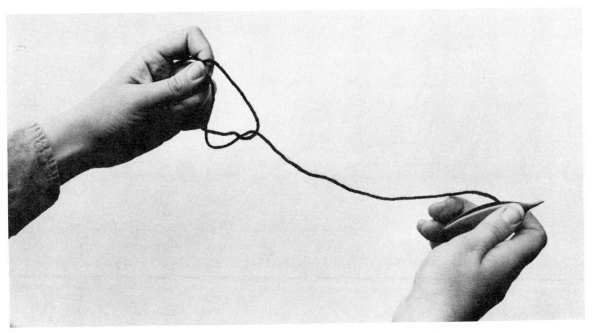

Relax fingers within loop, *pinching thumb and index finger firmly on joint.*

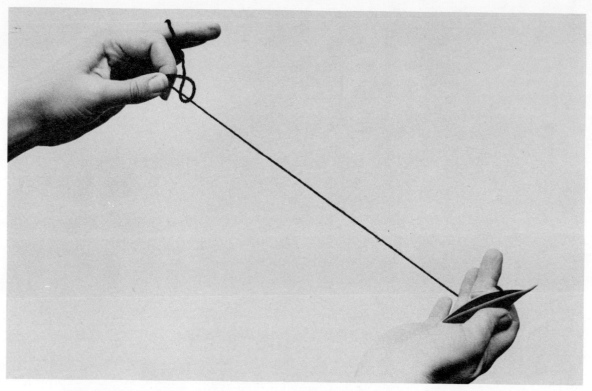

Pull firmly on shuttle thread. This will cause loop thread to change position and circle shuttle thread. Then slowly raise second and third fingers, bringing loop into position at base of ring (between thumb and forefinger) forming first part of stitch.

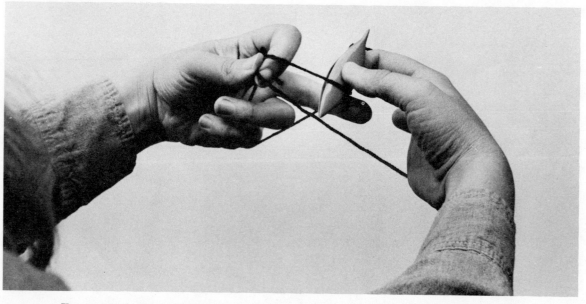

For second part of stitch, hold shuttle in right hand letting shuttle thread hang below it in a U. Pass tail of shuttle under far side of loop between index and second fingers, bringing shuttle toward you over the U of shuttle thread. Relax other fingers in loop.

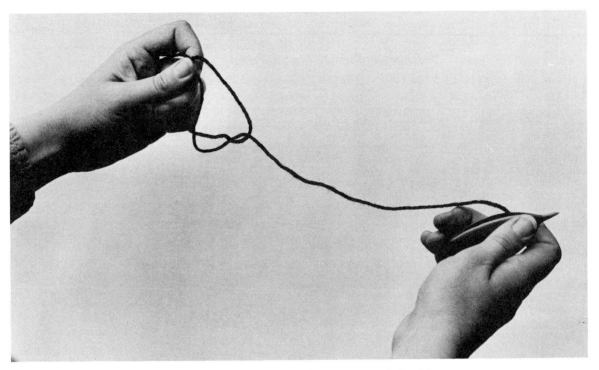

Pull shuttle thread, causing loop to turn right side up.

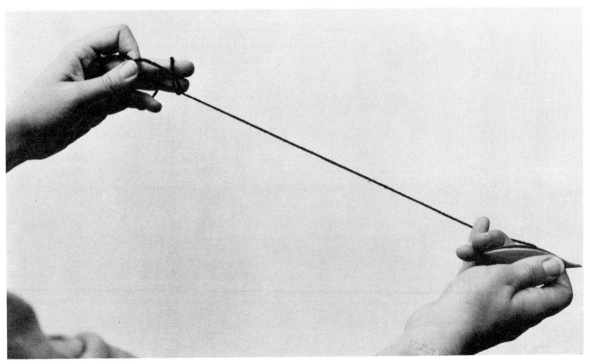

When loop is in right position spread loop fingers carefully bringing stitch into position beside first stitch at base of ring.

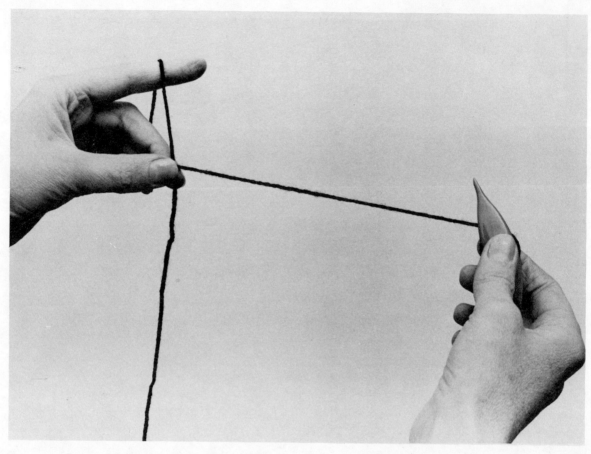

Loop shuttle thread loosely around right hand, pinching joint of loop between thumb and second finger. Hold shuttle in right hand, head held loosely between thumb and bottom of shuttle.

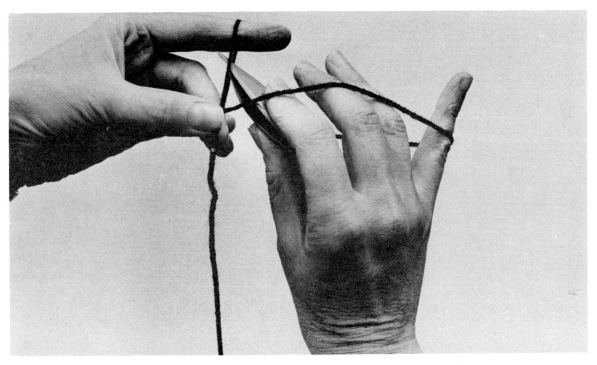

Pass shuttle under its own thread and under loop between thumb and second finger of left hand, with loop thread over top of shuttle.

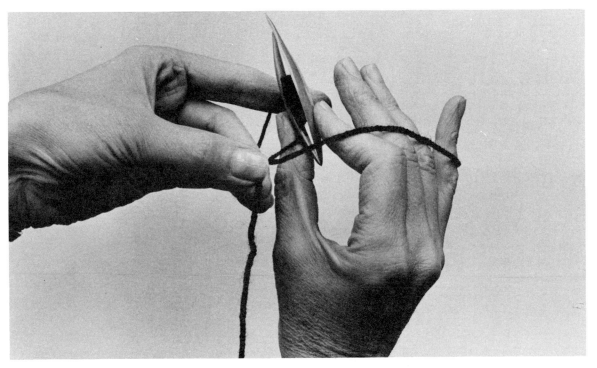

Slide loop thread first under index finger holding shuttle, then over tail of shuttle. Pull shuttle back out over loop with loop passing between thumb and bottom of shuttle.

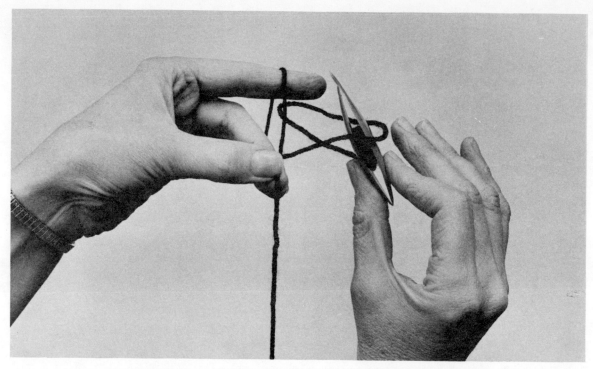

Shuttle will pass inside thread that runs over back of hand.

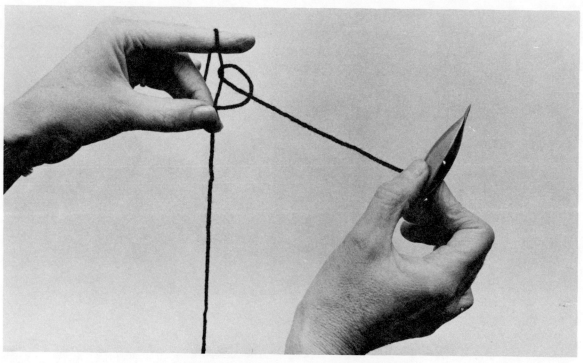

Loop will begin to form upside down.

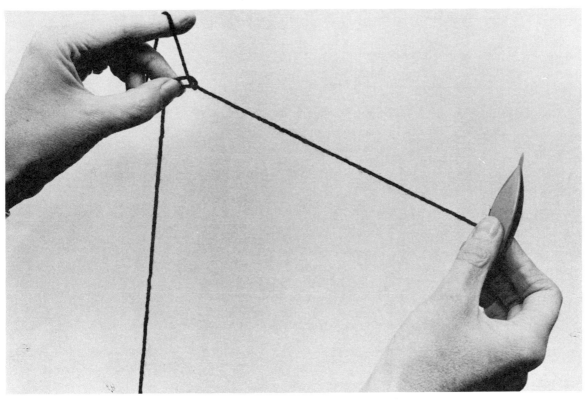

Relax index finger of left hand and pull shuttle thread so loop will form right side up. Pull into position at base of ring. This completes first stitch.

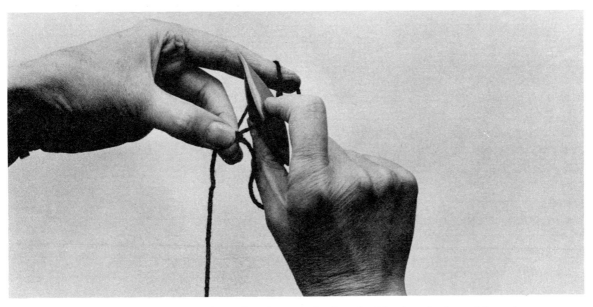

Begin second stitch holding shuttle in right hand with shuttle thread hanging below it in a U. Bring shuttle in from far side of loop (the side away from you), toward you with loop thread passing between index finger and top of shuttle.

Loop will begin to form upside down.

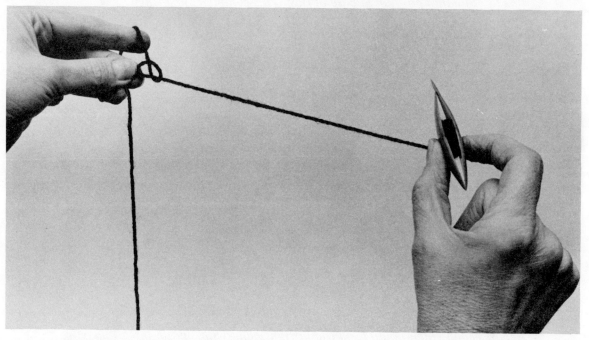

Relax index finger of left hand and pull on shuttle thread, turning loop right side up. Bring second stitch into place beside first.

OTHER TATTING TECHNIQUES

Picots

Picots are made by leaving a length of loop thread between double stitches. They are useful for anchoring rings to rings and/or chains, and also serve to ornament.

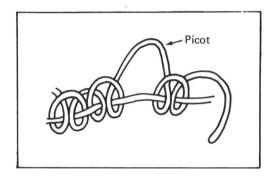

Picot between Double Stitches

Chains

Chains are worked from the bases of rings, like Ball and Chain edging (page 41), or may be connected to other chains in a netlike design, such as the "Free-form Rug" (page 65). It is easier for beginners to start by tying a ball thread to the base of a ring. Pinch knot at ring base between thumb and index finger of left hand. Spread fingers of left hand and run thread from the ball over backs of fingers, anchoring by winding 3 times around the first joint of little finger. Work shuttle between index and second fingers in exactly the same manner as for the ring. As thread is worked on left hand, take on more thread from ball of yarn, reanchoring around little finger. On heavy yarns it is sometimes possible to anchor thread in bend of little finger.

Classic Method For Making Chain

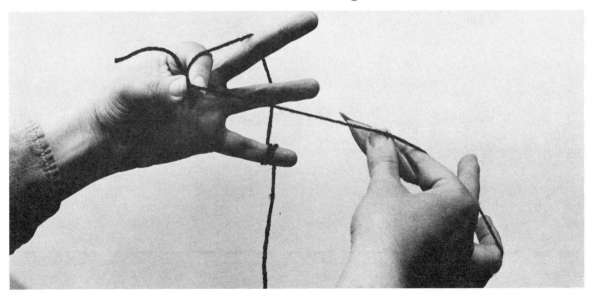

Tie ball and shuttle threads together. Pinch knot between thumb and index finger of left hand. Spread fingers of left hand and run ball thread over backs of fingers, anchoring by winding around the first joint of little finger. Work shuttle between index and second fingers in exactly the same manner as for ring.

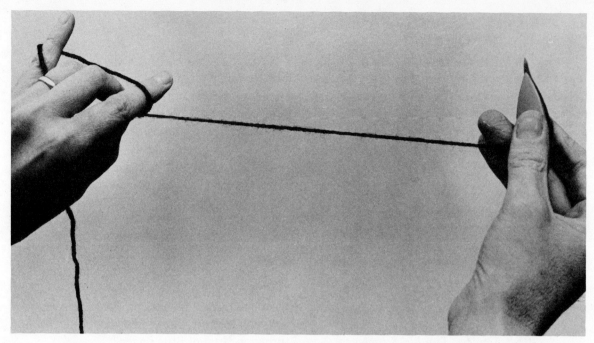

Tie ball and shuttle threads together and pinch knot between thumb and second finger of left hand. Spread fingers of left hand and run ball thread over backs of fingers, anchoring around little finger (photo credit: Norma Bowkett).

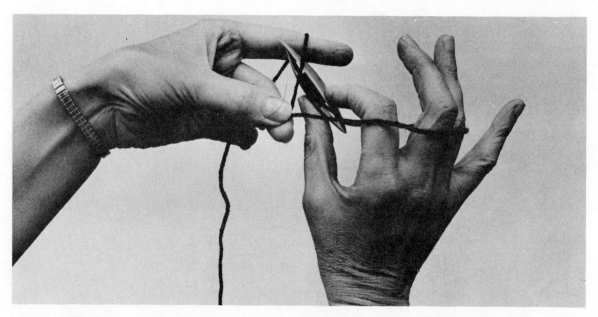

Work shuttle between thumb and index fingers in exactly the same method as for ring.

The Ludicrous Lion

Free-form rug

Bella—the Tatted Turtle

Beaded hemp necklace

Garden of Eden

Evening purse

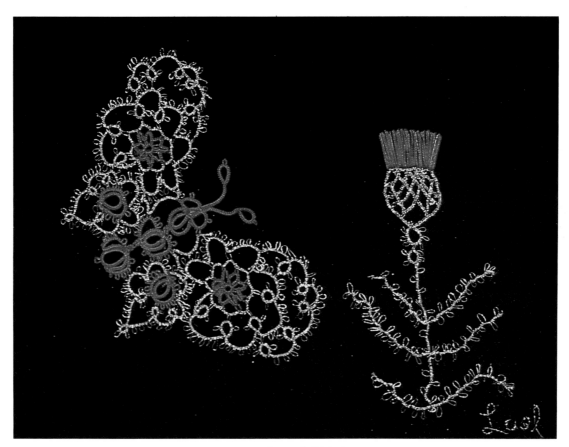

Butterfly and Thistle

Lace bodice top

Bulky trim for robe

Old-fashioned neck edging

Joining Work to Picot

With a hook pull thread that comes from top of stitch just completed through picot with which you wish to join, then pass shuttle through loop thus formed. Relax fingers of left hand and pull firmly on shuttle thread until the joining thread runs over shuttle thread as a stitch would. Open fingers of left hand and bring into place as you would a stitch.

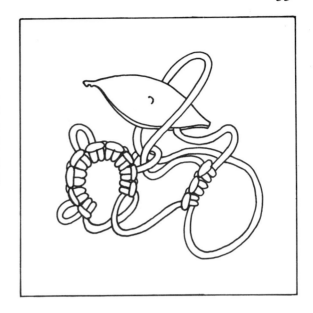

Joining work to Picot

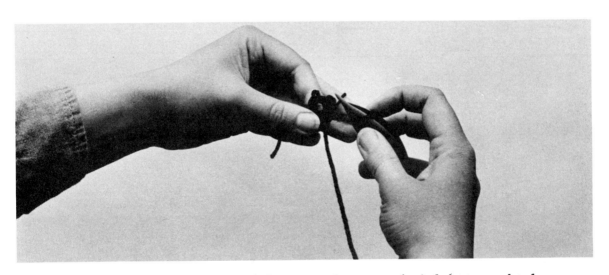

With hook or pick pull thread that comes from top of stitch just completed through picot with which you wish to join, then pass shuttle through loop formed. Relax fingers of left hand and pull firmly on joining thread runs over shuttle thread as a stitch would (photo credit: Norma Bowkett).

Joining Threads

A square knot is generally used for joining threads. For extra strength, work ends of knotted thread into next couple of stitches before clipping. In working slippery thread that does not knot well, anchor knots with needle and fine thread for added security.

Joining Beads

Large centered beads may be joined to lace with a crochet hook in the same manner as you would join work to a picot. Beads with centers too small for a hook may be joined by using a small needle and thread. Draw needle and thread through bead, circle lace thread to be joined, then pull needle and thread back through bead bringing with them a loop of lace thread to be joined. Pass shuttle through this loop.

Unraveling Mistakes

Because each tatting double-stitch locks, it is hard to undo mistakes. A pin or needle is usually needed for fine work.

If a ring has been made, it will be difficult to widen it back to a loop again. Begin by pushing the last two or three double stitches made to the base of the loop and work stitches made earlier toward them a few at a time. If this is not done carefully, the last stitch made will turn upside down, locking and jamming the loop. Once you are sure stitches are running free and you have enough loop thread at the base of the ring to get a hold on, pull it opening the noose.

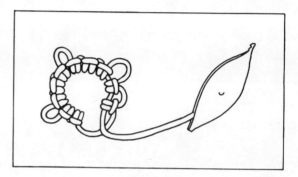

Undoing Ring

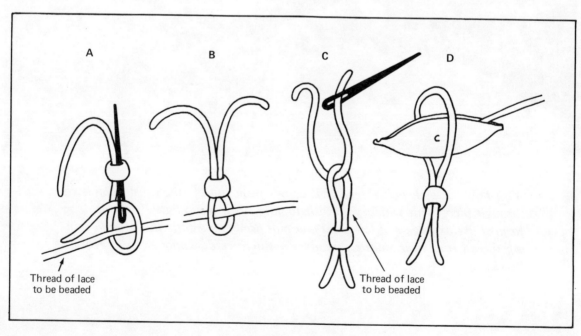

Joining small beads

Adding Bead To Ring, Step by Step

Pull thread that comes from top of stitch through bead and put shuttle thread through that loop.

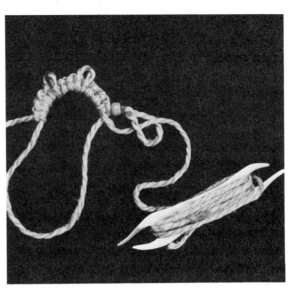

Pull loop that runs through bead closed.

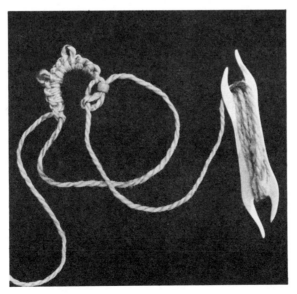

As loop closes work it to inside of ring. Put it in place as a regular stitch.

THE INDEPENDENT TATTER

Tatters in training should begin with a simple edging like Running Rings or Ball and Chain (page 42). The classic method with traditional shuttle is recommended at this point, along with crochet cotton thread which is widely available. Some manufacturers still produce tatting thread, which is usually quite fine. This is all right for beginners as it is tightly spun and will not fuzz, but I prefer to teach with a heavier weight crochet thread (Double-quick, 8-cord cable twist is lovely), which is easier to see and faster to work.

Once a beginner has mastered the basic knot and the mechanics of fringes, chains, and joinings, the world is hers/his. While some prefer to take simple patterns, step-by-step—others opt for freedom and "eyeball" it. Experienced tatters seldom follow written tatting directions unless the pattern is new to them and complicated. Generally, a look at the original will suffice, and many go at it with the idea of improving on the design.

For this reason, you don't often find directions for tatted clothing written for more than one size. If the garment is medium and you are large, it's assumed you will work a few more rows, adding a double stitch or two for each row and/or loop as the garment grows.

To me, though, the real joy of tatting is experimentation; not only with new designs but new materials and new equipment. Give me some manila hemp, some wrapping string,

dental floss—I'll try it. Piano wire, why not?

To accommodate various weights and types of "thread," I found I had to develop my own shuttle. A larger shuttle, with wider openings at either end made it much easier to work with materials like hemp or heavy yarn. Because of the size of the yarn shuttle, when tatting you must make minor adjustments in the classic method, although the technique is basically the same.

What set me off was the Queen of Romania who wrote of tatting thread spun of gold with beads of turquoise. Heady stuff! I'd never seen tatting that incorporated beads and the Queen didn't divulge her technique, but in a year or so I'd developed my own and was on my way.

My budget couldn't accommodate 12K gold thread (I figured 14K would not be malleable enough to do the job), but I did discover gold sewing machine thread worked as well; perhaps better. And it also comes in silver.

I learned the hard way that gold yarns and crochet threads are usually useless for tatting because their metal cover is wound around a base thread of cotton and comes off when pulled through the nooselike rings. I did find a marvelously soft French yarn—very expensive but worth every cent—that works well and looks so inviting that when I work on it on airplanes fellow passengers come to ask what I'm doing and to watch it sparkle.

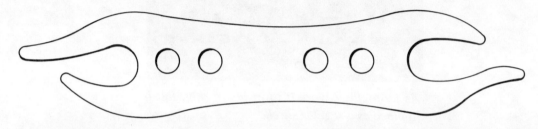

Large tatting shuttle—this shuttle can be cut from any strong material that will not easily bend when held. A ⅛-inch thickness is a good size.

Working Yarn Shuttle, Step by Step
(Photo credit: Ellen Wolf)

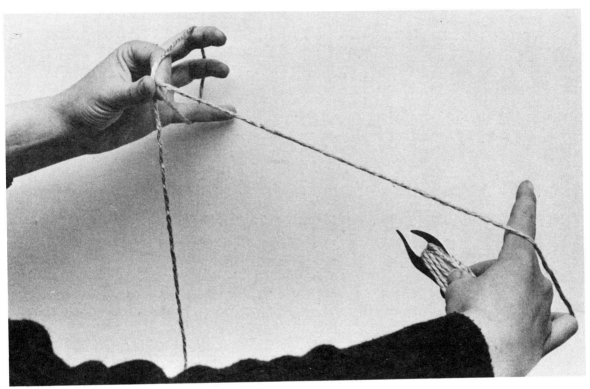

Grip shuttle below center and run shuttle thread from tail over back of hand.

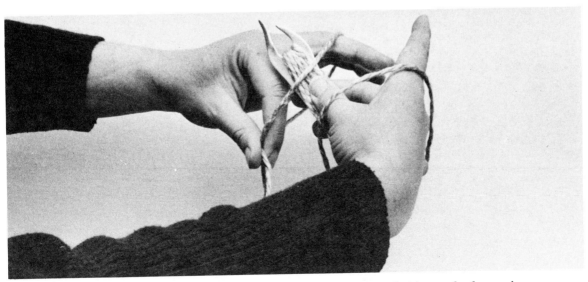

Work shuttle through loop in same direction as for classic method, moving fingers along shuttle for thrust.

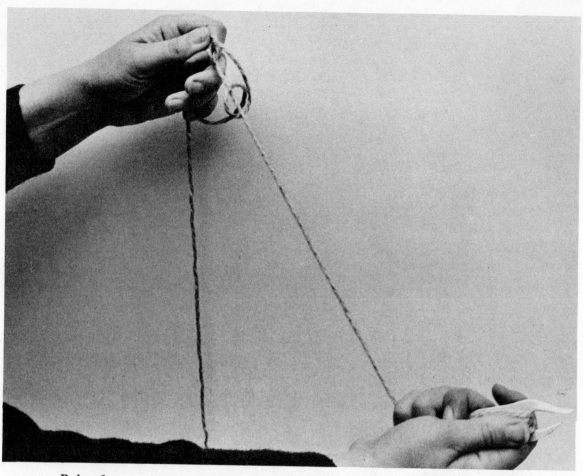

Relax fingers of left hand once shuttle leaves loop and pull on shuttle thread so knot will form right side up.

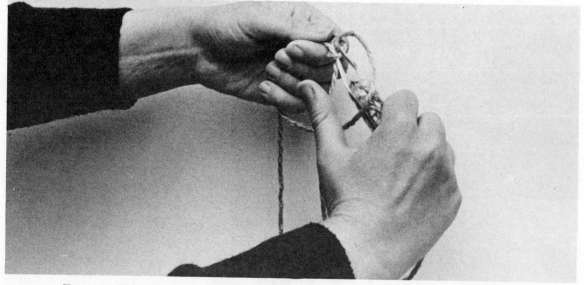

For second stitch work shuttle from palm to thumb as it goes through loop in same route as for classic method.

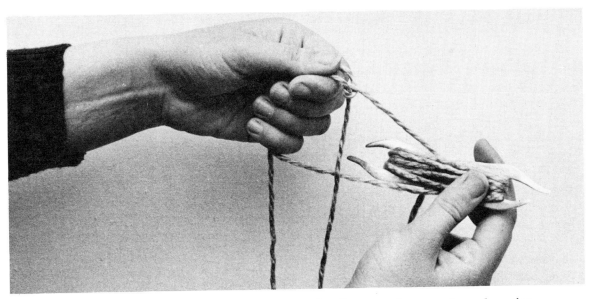

Maneuver shuttle between thumb and index finger as it comes from loop for second stitch. Relax fingers within the loop and pull on shuttle thread.

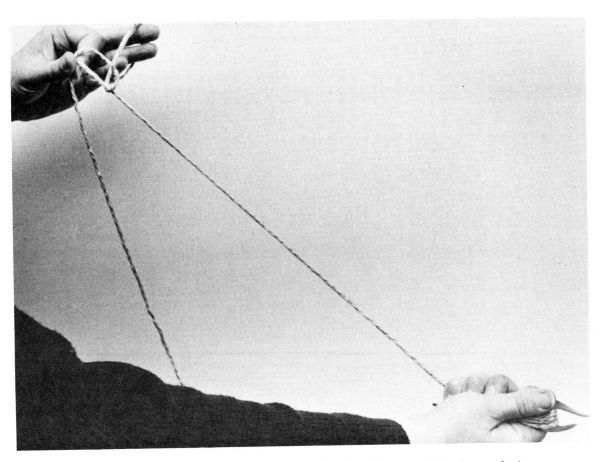

Keep firm pressure on shuttle thread and raise fingers within loop placing second stitch beside first.

Glossy embroidery floss serves for fine work and is a handsome accompaniment for fine gold. Nylon fish-net twine has great sheen, is strong and easy to tat, but cut ends ravel if you so much as look at them. To secure nylon you must melt it. I worked a carry-all bag (page 57) of heavy nylon net twine with a cigarette lighter handy, but figured the results worth the cooking.

Yarn is a field in itself. Rug yarn tats quickly and well with a large shuttle, but other heavy yarns may be too fuzzy to work freely. Once I got the bright idea of working pussy willows of mohair . . . possible but not practical. Sneezed for a week.

Fine baby yarn tats beautifully if it's not too fuzzy, and often it is practical to use it with the standard-size shuttle. Choose one with a removable bobbin, though. With a one-piece shuttle with boat-shaped ends, yarn tends to catch as you wind and looks used before it is ever worked.

The main thing to keep in mind is not to buy too much of any new material until you've tested it. The next item I'm considering as a tatting possibility is "diamonds by the yard," and I guess that goes without saying.

As for designing basics, there are only a couple to keep in mind. Too many decorative picots on a functional piece of clothing tend to turn, twist, and look messy. This kind of work is best left for doilies and heavily starched pieces or wall hangings that can be permanently anchored. On the other hand, patterns that are too holey with gaping chains and large, picotless rings, will not serve for rugs or placemats where a firm base is needed.

If speed is of the essence, remember you can always cheat with chains. They work much faster than rings and, because they require a minimum of shuttle thread, they mean less shuttle winding and fewer knots.

Of course, the ultimate lazy man's space-filling design is the net pattern which utilizes a length of unknotted string instead of chain and features lots of air. If there were a Tatting Olympics where speed counted, I'd go with the net pattern. Otherwise, it's well to remember that quality, not quantity, best suits the independent tatter.

III

Traditional Designs

EDGINGS

Running Rings

Ring of 6ds, 3p separated by 6ds each, 6ds, close. *Ring of 6ds, join to last p of last ring, 6ds, p, 6ds, p, 6ds, close.** Repeat from * for desired length.

Three-quarter Running Rings

Ring of 2ds, 5p separated by 1ds each, 2ds, close three quarters of the way, leaving ¼" thread at open base. *Ring of 2ds, join to last p of last ring, 1ds, 4p separated by 1ds each, 2ds, close three quarters of the way, leaving ¼" thread at open base.** Repeat from * for desired length.

Hopscotch

*Ring of 5ds, p, 2ds, p, 2ds, close. Leave ¹⁄₁₆" of thread. Ring of 2ds, join to last p of last ring, 2ds, p, 5ds, close. RW. Ring of 5ds, p, 2ds, p, 2ds, close. Leave ¹⁄₁₆" of thread. Ring of 2ds, join to last p of last ring, 2ds, p, 5ds, close. RW.** Repeat from * for desired length.

Double Running Rings

Ring of 3ds, 5p separated by 1ds each, 3ds, close. RW. Ring of 3ds, 5p separated by 1ds each, 3ds, close. *RW. Ring of 3ds, join to last p of ring before last, 1ds, 4p separated by 1ds each, 3ds, close.** Repeat from * for desired length.

Clover

Ring of 11ds, p, 7ds, p, 3ds, close. *Ring of 3ds, join to last p of last ring, 8ds, p, 7ds, p, 3ds, close. Ring of 3ds, join to last p of last ring, 8ds, p, 7ds, p, 3ds, close. Leave about ¾" of thread. Ring of 11ds, join to center p of last ring, 7ds, p, 3ds, close.** Repeat from * for desired length.

Ball and Chain

Tie ball and shuttle threads together. Ring of 6ds, p, 4ds, p, 4ds, p, 6ds, close. *RW. Chain of 6ds, p, 6ds. RW. Ring of 6ds, join to last p of last ring, 4ds, p, 4ds, p, 6ds, close.** Repeat from * for desired length.

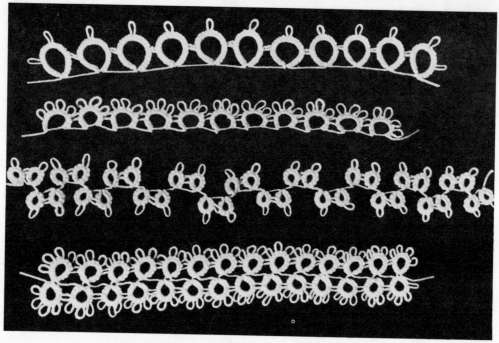

Above: Running Rings
Second from top: Three-quarter Running Rings
Third from top: Hopscotch
Below: Double Running Rings

Above: Clover
Second from top: Ball and Chain
Third from top: Dewdrop
Below: Frieze

Dewdrop

Ring of 6ds, p, 4ds, p, 4ds, p, 6ds, close. *RW. Ring of 5ds, p, 5ds, close. RW. Ring of 6ds, join to last p of next-to-last ring, 4ds, p, 4ds, p, 6ds, close. RW. Ring of 5ds, join to p on next-to-last ring, 1ds, 6p separated by 1ds each, 5ds, close. RW. Ring of 6ds, join to last p on next-to-last ring, 4ds, p, 4ds, p, 6ds, close. RW. Ring of 5ds, join to last p of next-to-last ring, 5ds, close. RW. Ring of 6ds, join to last p of next-to-last ring, 4ds, p, 4ds, p, 6ds, close.** Repeat from * for desired length.

Frieze

Tie ball and shuttle threads together. Ring of 3ds, 3p separated by 1ds each, 5ds, close. RW. Chain of 3ds, 5p separated by 1ds each, join to 1st p of ring. *RW. Chain of 3ds, 5p separated by 1ds each, join to 3rd p of last chain.** Repeat from * for desired length. Can be ended with a 2d ring.

Mixed Bouquet

Tie ball and shuttle threads together. Chain of 2ds, 5p separated by 1ds each, 2ds, p, 3ds. RW. Ring of 3ds, 3p separated by 3ds each, 3ds, close. Ring of 3ds, join to last p of last ring, 3ds, p, 3ds, p, 3ds, close. *Ring of 3ds, join to last p of last ring, 1ds, 6p separated by 1ds each, 3ds, close. Ring of 3ds, join to last p of last ring, 3ds, p, 3ds, p, 3ds, close. Ring of 3ds, join to last p of last ring, 3ds, p, 3ds, p, 3ds, close. RW. Chain of 3ds, join to last p of last chain, 2ds, 5p separated by 1ds each, 2ds, p. RW. Chain of 6ds, join to center p of next-to-last ring, 4ds. RW. Ring of 3ds, 3p separated by 3ds each, 3ds, close. RW. Chain of 4ds, p, 6ds, join to next-to-last p of last chain, 2ds, 5p separated by 1ds each, 2ds, p, 2ds. RW. Ring of 3ds, p, 3ds, join to last p of next-to-last chain, 3ds, p, 3ds, close. Ring of 3ds, join to last p of last ring, 3ds, p, 3ds, p, 3ds, close. Ring of 3ds, join to last p of last ring, 3ds, p, 3ds, p, 3ds, close. RW. Chain of 2ds, join to last p of last chain, 2ds, 5p separated by 1ds each, 2ds, p. RW. Chain of 6ds, join to center p of last ring, 4ds. RW. Ring of 3ds, 3p separated by 3ds each, 3ds, close. RW. Chain of 4ds, p, 6ds, join to next-to-last p of last chain. Chain of 2ds, 5p separated by 1ds each, 2ds, p, 3ds. RW. Ring of 3ds, 3p separated by 3ds each, 3ds, close. Ring of 3ds, join to last p

Above: Mixed Bouquet
Middle: Anchor trim
Below: Fat Leaf

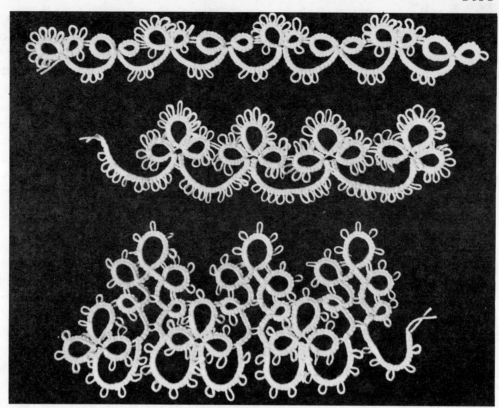

Above: Sweet and Sour
Middle: Fancy Clover
Below: Grapevine

of last ring, 3ds, join to last p next-to-last chain, 3ds, p, 3ds, close.** Repeat from * for desired length.

Anchor Trim

Tie ball and shuttle threads together. Ring of 3ds, 3p separated by 3ds each, 3ds, close. *RW. Chain of 5ds, p, 4ds, p, 2ds, p, 4ds. RW. Ring of 4ds, join to last p of last ring, 2p separated by 3ds each, 4ds, close. Ring of 4ds, join to last p of last ring, 3ds, 4p separated by 3ds each, 4ds, close. Ring of 4ds, join to last p of last ring, 3ds, p, 3ds, p, 4ds, close. RW. Chain of 4ds, join to last p of last chain, 2ds, join to next p of last chain, 4ds, p, 5ds. RW. Ring of 4ds, join to last p of last ring, 3ds, p, 3ds, p, 4ds, close. RW. Chain of 5ds, p, 5ds. RW. Ring of 4ds, join to last p of last ring, 3ds, p, 3ds, p, 4ds, close. RW.** Repeat from * for desired length.

Fat Leaf

Tie ball and shuttle threads together. Ring of 4ds, p, 4ds, close. RW. Ring of 3ds, 9p separated by 3ds each, 3ds. RW. Chain of 8ds, p, 3ds, p, 4ds. RW. *Ring of 4ds, join to 8th p of last ring, 4ds, close. RW. Chain of 3ds, 5p separated by 3ds each, 3ds. RW. Ring of 4ds, join to 6th p of next-to-last ring, 4ds, close. RW. Chain of 4ds, p, 3ds, p, 8ds, join to 4th p of largest ring. Ring of 4ds, p, 4ds, close. RW. Chain of 8ds. RW. Ring of 4ds, p, 4ds, close. RW. Ring of 3ds, 9p separated by 3ds each, 3ds, close. RW. Chain of 8ds, join to last p of next-to-last chain, 3ds, p, 4ds. RW.** Repeat from * for desired length.

Sweet and Sour

Tie ball and shuttle threads together. Ring of 3ds, 9p, 3ds, close. *RW. Ring of 3ds, join to last p of last ring, 1ds, 4p separated by 1ds each, 2ds, close. RW. Chain of 6ds, 3p, 6ds. RW. Ring of 9ds, join to next-to-last p of last ring, 9ds, close. RW. Ring of 6ds, p, 6ds, close. RW. Chain of 6ds, 3p, 6ds. RW. Ring of 3ds, p, join to p of last ring, 1ds, 7p, 3ds, close.** Repeat from * for desired length.

Fancy Clover

Tie ball and shuttle threads together. Chain of 5ds, 5p, 3ds, 5p, 3ds, p, 2ds. RW. Ring of 5ds, 7p, 5ds, close. *Ring of 5ds, join to last p of last ring, 1ds, 8p, 5ds, close. Ring of 5ds, join to last p of last ring, 1ds, 6p, 5ds, close. RW. Chain of 2ds, join to last p of last chain, 3ds, 5p, 3ds, 5p, 3ds, p, 2ds. RW. Ring of 5ds, 3p, join to center p of last ring, 1ds, 3p, 5ds, close.** Repeat from * for desired length.

Grapevine

Tie ball and shuttle threads together. Ring of 3ds, 5p separated by 3ds each, 3ds, close. Ring of 3ds, join to last p of last ring, 6p separated by 3ds each, 3ds, close. *Ring of 3ds, join to last p of last ring, 4p separated by 3ds each, 3ds, close. RW. Chain of 3ds, 6p separated by 3ds each, 3ds, join to center p of last ring. Chain of 3ds, p, 4ds. RW. Ring of 3ds, p, 3ds,

join to 5th p of 2nd ring, 3ds, p, 3ds, close. RW. Chain of 3ds, p, 3ds. RW. Ring of 3ds, join to last p of last ring, 3ds, 4p separated by 3ds each, 3ds, close. RW. Chain of 3ds. RW. Ring of 3ds, join to last p of last ring, 3ds, 6p separated by 3ds each, 3ds, close. RW. Chain of 3ds. RW. Ring of 3ds, join to last p of last ring, 3ds, 4p separated by 3ds each, 3ds, close. RW. Chain of 3ds, join to last chain with a p, 3ds. RW. Ring of 3ds, join to last p of last ring, 3ds, 2p separated by 3ds each, 3ds, close. RW. Chain of 4ds, join to p of next chain opposite, 6ds, 6p separated by 3ds each, 3ds. RW. Ring of 3ds, p, 3ds, p, 3ds, join between 3rd and 4th ds of last ring on inside, 3ds, p, 3ds, p, 3ds, close. Ring of 3ds, join to last p of last ring, 3ds, p, 3ds, join to center p of next to last ring, 3ds, 3p separated by 3ds each, 3ds, close.** Repeat from * for desired length.

Rolling Rings

Tie ball and shuttle threads together. Ring of 2ds, 7p separated by 2ds each, 2ds, close. RW. Chain of 3ds, 7p separated by 2ds each, 3ds, join to center p of last ring. *RW. Ring of 2ds, 7p separated by 2ds each, 2ds, close. RW. Chain of 3ds, join to last p of last chain, 2ds, 6p separated by 2ds each, 3ds.** Repeat from * for desired length.

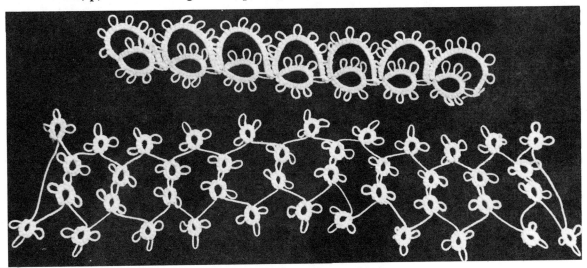

Above: Rolling Rings
Below: Double-ringed net

Double-ringed Net

Round 1: *Ring of 2ds, 3p separated by 2ds each, 2ds, close. RW. Leave ¼" thread.** Repeat from * for desired length, figuring ¼" between every other ring as top of row. Do not cut thread. Leave 1", and RW to begin 2nd round.

Round 2: *Ring of 2ds, 3p separated by 2ds each, 2ds, close. Leave ½" thread. Ring of 2ds, p, 2ds, join to center p of next-to-last ring round 1, 2ds, p, 2ds, close. RW. Leave ½" thread.** Repeat from * along bottom of Round 1. Additional rounds may be added using directions for round 2 for wider edging.

Smocked Rickrack

MATERIALS: ⚹30 crochet thread and baby rickrack. *Ring of 4ds, p, 4ds, close. RW. Leave less than ¼" thread.** Repeat from * for desired length counting every other ring as width. Sew p of every other ring to bottom hills, top bar of rickrack. The p of the remain-ing rings should be sewed to the top hills, bottom bar of rickrack.

Double-flowered Rickrack

MATERIALS: ⚹30 crochet thread and jumbo rickrack. Tie ball and shuttle threads together. Sew to beginning top hill of rickrack. *Chain of 7ds. Ring of 1ds, 5p, 1ds, close. RW. Ring of 1ds, 5p, 1ds, close. Chain of 7ds. Sew to next hill, top of rickrack.** Repeat from * for desired length.

Ball-and-chain Rickrack

MATERIALS: ⚹30 crochet thread and jumbo rickrack. Tie ball and shuttle threads together and sew to beginning top hill of rickrack. *Chain of 4ds, p, 4ds. RW. Ring of 5ds, p, 5ds, close. Sew p of ring to next depression top of rickrack. RW. Chain of 4ds, p, 4ds. Sew to next hill, top of rickrack.** Repeat from * for desired length. Also repeat pattern to trim bottom of rickrack.

Above: Smocked rickrack
Middle: Double-flowered rickrack
Below: Ball and Chain rickrack

RIBBON INSERTS FOR DOTTED SWISS

MATERIALS: Approximately 9 yards of 1"-wide looped ribbon with 6 loops to the inch. One skein light crochet cotton (Bucilla super-mercerized Wondersheen ✂11). Choose dress pattern and cut 4 ribbon lengths to match width of skirt.

Narrow Band for Top Inset: Ring of 4ds, p, 4ds, join to 4th loop of top ribbon, 4ds, p, 4ds, close. RW. At base of 1st ring make 2nd ring the same pattern joining center p to 4th loop of bottom ribbon. *RW. Leave ¼" of thread. Ring of 4ds, join to the last p of last ring top (1st ring), 4ds, join to 3rd loop from last joined loop top ribbon (6 loops from beginning), 4ds, p, 4ds, close. RW. At base of last ring make ring of 4ds, join to last p of next-to-last ring, 4ds, join to 3rd loop from last joined loop bottom ribbon (6 loops from beginning), 4ds, p, 4ds, close.** Repeat from * joining center p of each r to every other loop of ribbons.

Wide Band for Bottom Inset: Same pattern as for narrow band except made 2 rows deep. Make first tatting row joined to top ribbon *only*. Join second row to bottom of first row, then to bottom ribbon.

Ribbon inserts for dotted swiss

Ribbon inserts for dotted swiss (detail)

BOW TIE

MATERIAL: Fine tatting thread (less than a spool). Scrap of fabric or ribbon for backing. Tie is approximately 3″, or about same size as a man's bow tie.

Center: Tie ball and shuttle threads together. Ring of 5ds, 5p separated by 1ds each, 5ds, close. RW. *Chain of 3ds, 3p separated by 3ds each, 3ds. RW. Ring of 5ds, join to last p of last ring, 4p separated by 1ds each, 5ds, close. RW.** Repeat from * once. RW. Chain of 5ds, join to last p of last ring, 11ds. RW. Ring of 5ds, join between 6th and 7th ds of last chain, 1ds, p, 1ds, join to center p of last ring, 1ds, p, 1ds, p, 5ds, close. *RW. Chain of 3ds, 3p separated by 3ds each, 3ds. RW. Ring of 5ds, join to last p of last ring, 1ds, p, 1ds, join to center p of opposite (2nd) ring, 1ds, p, 1ds, p, 5ds, close.** Repeat from * once. RW. Chain of 5ds, join to last p of last ring, 6ds, join to 1st p of 1st ring, 5ds, join to base of 1st ring. Tie and cut.

Round 1 (Left side): Tie ball and shuttle threads together. Ring of 5ds, p, 1ds, p, 1ds, join to 1st p of 1st chain center, 1ds, p, 1ds, p, 5ds, close. *RW. Chain of 3ds, p, 3ds. RW. Ring of 5ds, join to last p of last ring, 1ds, p, 1ds, join to next p (1st chain of center), 1ds, p, 1ds, p, 5ds, close. RW. Chain of 3ds, p, 3ds. RW. Ring of 5ds, join to last p of last ring, 1ds, p, 1ds, join to last p of 1st chain of center, join to 1st p 2nd chain of center, 1ds, p, 1ds, p, 5ds, close. Repeat pattern from * joining to last 2p of 2nd ring center. Tie and cut.

Round 2: Ring of 3ds, p, 3ds, join to base of 1st ring round 1, 3ds, p, 3ds, close. *RW. Chain of 2ds, 3p separated by 2ds each, 2ds. RW. Ring of 3ds, join to last p of last ring, 3ds, join to (1st) p (1st) chain round 1, 3ds, p, 3ds, close.** Repeat from * along round, anchoring center of last ring at base of last ring round 1. Tie and cut.

Round 3: Ring of 2ds, p, 2ds, join to 1st p 1st chain round 2, 2ds, p, 2ds, close (bottom). RW. Ring of 2ds, 5p separated by 1ds each, 2ds, close (top). *RW. Leave less than ¼″ thread. Ring of 2ds, join to last p of last bottom ring, 2ds, join to next p round 2, 2ds, p, 2ds, close. RW. Ring of 2ds, join to last p top ring, 4p separated by 1ds each, 2ds, close.** Repeat along round 2. Tie and cut. Work right side to correspond with left.

CONSTRUCTION: Cut ribbon or fabric with which to back tatted bow. Sew safety pin on back of center.

Bow tie

OLD-FASHIONED NECK EDGING WITH BUTTON LOOPS

MATERIALS: Fairly fine tatting thread. Small pearl buttons with wire base. (See color pages.)

Directions: Tie ball and shuttle threads together. *Make ring of 3ds, 3p separated by 3ds each, 3ds, close. RW. Make chain of 15ds. RW. Ring of 3ds, join to last p of 1st ring, 3ds, p, 3ds, p, 3ds, close. RW.** Repeat from * for width of collar ending with large chain looping over edge of front. Continue down right front with *ring of 3ds, join to last p of last ring, 3ds, p, 3ds, p, 3ds, close. RW. Chain of 12ds. RW. Ring of 3ds, join to last p of last ring, 3ds, p, 3ds, p, 3ds, close. RW. Chain of 15ds.** Repeat from * down dress front setting buttons on right side inside of the small chains. At base of neck opening make ring of 3ds, join to last p of last ring, 3ds, p, 3ds, p, 3ds. RW. Make chain of 16ds. RW. Ring of 3ds, 3p separated by 3ds each, 3ds, close. RW. Chain of 16ds. RW. Ring of 3ds, 3p separated by 3ds each, 3ds, close. RW. Chain of 12ds. RW. Ring of 3ds, join to last p of last ring, 3ds, p, 3ds, close. Work left front as you did right front, making sure large chains on left side are opposite buttons in small chains on right to serve as button loops.

Old-fashioned neck edging with button loops

APRON WITH LACE RIBBON TRIM

MATERIALS: Fine white crochet thread. One and one-half yards of cotton, 42″ wide. Six′ of narrow, loop-edged ribbon.

Apron with lace ribbon trim (*detail*)

Tatting Pattern: Cut ribbon into 2 3′ strips. Make ring of 3ds, p, 3ds, join to 4th loop on ribbon, 3ds, p, 3ds, close. RW. Chain of 5ds. RW. Ring of 3ds, p, 3ds, join to 7th loop on remaining ribbon, 3ds, p, 3ds, close. RW. Chain of 5ds. *RW. Ring of 3ds, join to last p of top (1st) ring, 3ds, join to 7th loop of top (1st) ribbon, 3ds, p, 3ds, close. RW. Chain of 5ds. RW. Ring of 3ds, join to last p of bottom (2nd) ring, 3ds, join to 10th loop on bottom ribbon, 3ds, p, 3ds, close.** Repeat from * attaching rings to ribbons with 2 loops between each for the length of ribbon, leaving edges for finishing.

CONSTRUCTION: Cut length of cotton 32″ long, leaving selvages for apron sides. Hem lower edge and sew ribbon loops to it. Cut another length about 5″ wide for apron bottom. Hem upper edge and sew ribbon loops on bottom of trim to it. Hem bottom to desired apron length. For waistband, cut a strip of cotton 5″×16″ wide, folding double so it measures 2½″×16″. Turn selvage in. Gather apron top to fit and sew to waistband. Add hemmed apron strings measuring about 42″×1¾″ on each side of waistband.

Apron with lace ribbon trim—dress features old-fashioned neck edging with button loops.

Toddler trim

TODDLER TRIM

MATERIALS: Regular-size rickrack and fine tatting thread. Needle and matching sewing thread.

Tie ball and shuttle threads together and anchor to top of beginning hill of rickrack. Chain of 7ds. *Ring of 2ds, 5p, 2ds, close. Chain of 7ds. Anchor to next top hill of rickrack.** Repeat from * for desired length.

IV

New Things to Do— Quick and Easy

BELLA—THE TATTED TURTLE

MATERIALS: One skein fingering yarn (Berella multicolored 1 oz.). Half-yard green felt for shell, legs, and head. Scrap of mustard felt for eyelid. Scrap of yellow felt for eye. Two shoe buttons for eyeballs. Black embroidery floss. Stuffing. Thread to match felt. (See color pages.)

Turtle Shell

Center: Ring of 2ds, 5p separated by 2ds each, close. Tie and cut.

Round 1: Tie ball and shuttle threads together. *Ring of 2ds, p, 2ds, join to p of 1st ring, 2ds, p, 2ds, close. RW. Chain of 2ds, 5 p separated by 1ds each, 2ds. RW.** Repeat from * around center ring ending by joining last (5th) chain at base of 1st ring round 1. Tie and cut.

Round 2: Tie ball and shuttle threads together. *Ring of 2ds, p, 2ds, join to 2nd p 1st chain round 1, 2ds, p, 2ds, close. RW. Chain of 2ds, 5 p separated by 1ds each, 2ds. RW.

Ring of 2ds, p, 2ds, join to 4th p 1st chain round 1, 2ds, p, 2ds, close. RW.** Repeat from * along round 1 joining rings to 2nd and 4th p of each chain round 1. Tie and cut.

Round 3: Repeat directions for round 2 along round 2. Tie and cut.

Round 4: Tie ball and shuttle threads together. *Ring of 2ds, p, 2ds, join to center p of 1st chain round 3, 2ds, p, 2ds, close. RW. Chain of 2ds, 5p separated by 1ds each, 2ds. RW.** Repeat from * along round 3 joining rings of round 4 to center p of each chain round 3. Tie and cut.

Round 5: Repeat directions for round 4, joining each ring of this round to center p of each chain round 4. Tie and cut.

Round 6: Repeat directions for round 2 joining ring of this round in 2nd and 4th p of chains round 5. Tie and cut.

Turtle Cap

Tie ball and shuttle threads together. Ring of 2ds, 3p separated by 2ds each, 2ds, close.

Bella—the Tatted Turtle

RW. Chain of 2ds, 8p separated by 1ds each, 2ds. RW. Ring of 2ds, p, 2ds, join to center p last ring, 2ds, p, 2ds, close. RW. Chain of 2ds, 3p separated by 1ds each, 2ds. RW. Ring of 2ds, join to last p of last ring, 2ds, p, 2ds, p, 2ds, close. RW. Chain of 2ds, 7p separated by 1ds each, 2ds. RW. Ring of 2ds, p, 2ds, join to center p of last ring, 2ds, join to 1st p of 1st ring, 2ds, close. RW. Chain of 2ds, 3p separated by 1ds, each, 2ds, join to base of 1st ring. Tie and cut.

Ears

Ring of 2ds, 3p, separated by 1ds each, 2ds, close. Ring of 2ds, join to last p of last ring, 1ds, p, 1ds, p, 2ds, close. Ring of 2ds, join to last p of last ring, 1ds, p, 1ds, p, 2ds, close. Ring of 2ds, join to last p of last ring, 1ds, p, 1ds, join to 1st p of 1st ring, 2ds, close. Tie and cut. Repeat for 2nd ear.

CONSTRUCTION: The turtle is made from green felt. To form body, cut 2 circles, each 9½" in diameter. Trace the patterns for the other turtle parts, cutting the number of pieces indicated. Stitch 3 pieces of head together and turn right side out, seam in. Stuff head. Sew mustard eyelids on yellow eye pieces and add eyelashes in black blanket stitch. Sew eyes on head. Sew on shoe buttons in corners of eyes. Embroider mouth with black stem stitch. Stitch on tatted cap and ears. Stitch tatted shell to felt shell top. Embroider toes in stem stitch. Stitch top of legs to bottom shell. Stitch front insert pieces to either side of neck, seam in. Stitch tail between seam of 2 back insert pieces. Stitch this combined piece to shell bottom, seam out. Stitch head and front inserts to shell bottom, seam out. Stitch upper part of head and front to upper shell and upper part of back to upper shell, then seam top and bottom shells together on side leaving just enough room to stuff. When turtle is firmly filled, close final gap. (Shell seams are on outside, raw edges out.)

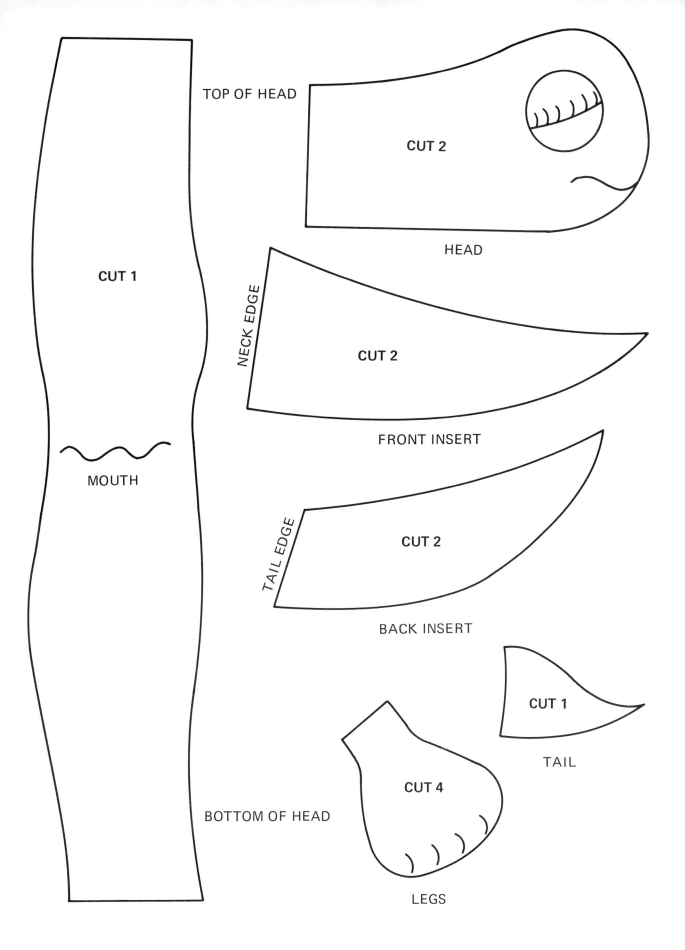

TOP OF HEAD

CUT 2

HEAD

CUT 1

NECK EDGE

CUT 2

FRONT INSERT

MOUTH

TAIL EDGE

CUT 2

BACK INSERT

CUT 1

TAIL

CUT 4

BOTTOM OF HEAD

LEGS

LACE-APPLIQUÉD BABY BOOTS

MATERIALS: One pair plain baby booties and fine tatting thread.

Top Trim: Ring of 4ds, 3p separated by 4ds each, 4ds, close (top). *RW. Leave ¼" thread. Ring of 4ds, p, 4ds, close (bottom). RW. Leave ¼" thread. Ring of 4ds, join to last p of last ring of top, 4ds, p, 4ds, p, 4ds, close. RW. Leave ½" thread. Ring of 4ds, p, 4ds, close. Leave ½" thread. Ring of 4ds, join to last p of last ring of top, 4ds, p, 4ds, p, 4ds, close.** Repeat from * around top of each boot. Tie and cut.

Toe Trim: Ring of 1ds, 4p separated by 1ds each, close. *Leave ½" thread. Ring of 1ds, 4p separated by 1ds each, close.** Repeat from * 4 times. Tie and cut. *Ring of 1ds, 4p separated by 1ds each, close. Tie and cut.** Repeat from * twice. (Duplicate above trim directions for toe of second boot.)

CONSTRUCTION: Sew top trim to boots with only top picots above the boot edge. Appliqué toe trim as shown with string of flowers grouped toward instep and three flowers floating free on outside of each boot toe. End of each boot lace may be trimmed with ring of 1ds, 4p separated by 1ds each, close. Tie and cut.

STRING BAG

MATERIALS: One plain tote bag. Heavy string. (I used heavyweight nylon-net line. It is unusually strong and pretty, but has the disadvantage of raveling unless each cut is sealed by heat.)

Round 1: *Ring of 6ds, p, 6ds, close (top). RW. Leave 2" of string. Ring of 4ds, p, 4ds, close (bottom). RW. Leave 2" of string. RW.** Repeat from * until you have enough large rings to space evenly around mouth of bag to serve as holders for draw string. Leave 2" of string and anchor at base of 1st ring. Tie and cut.

Round 2: Tie string in p of any of small rings round 1. Leave 2" of string. *Ring of 4ds, p, 4ds, close. Leave 2" of string. Anchor in p of next small ring round 1. Leave 2" of string.** Repeat from * along round 1, anchoring last 2" length of string in p of 1st small ring round 1. Tie and cut.

Additional Length: Repeat round 2 until you reach the bottom of the bag. Sew p of bottom row firmly to seam of bag bottom.

Lace-appliquéd baby boots

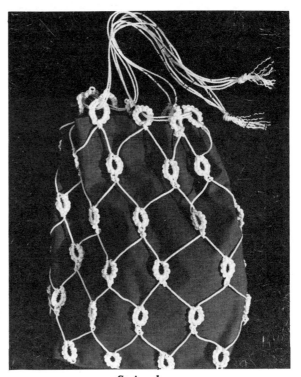

String bag

PILLOW BOUQUET

MATERIALS: Leftover yarn in flower shades. Round, 12″ pillow covered with dark velvet.

Basic Flower: Make ring of 1ds, 5p separated by 1ds each, close. Tie and cut. Tie ball and shuttle threads together and join to 1st p of ring. *Chain of 1ds, 4p, 1ds, join to next p of ring.** Repeat from * around ring, joining end of last chain to 1st p. Tie and cut.

Work 6 more flowers of contrasting colors, joining 2 center p of a chain of the first flower to 2 center p of a chain of each additional flower and joining additional flowers to each other in the same manner. Tie and cut.

Center on pillow and sew down.

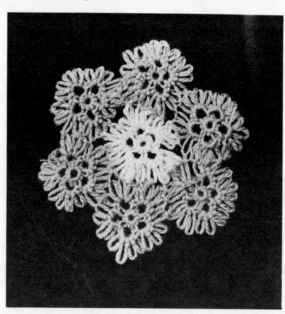

Pillow boutique

FANCY DAN DOG COLLAR

MATERIALS: About 12″ ¾″-wide grosgrain ribbon (hot pink). Velcro self-gripping fastener, ½″. Silk tatting thread (purple). Decorative bead.

Basic Trim: Ring of 8ds, 5p separated by 1ds each, 8ds, close. *Leave ½″ thread. Ring of 8ds, join to last p of last ring, 1ds, 4p separated by 1ds each, 8ds, close.** Repeat from * for length of collar.

Center Decoration: Ring of 8ds, 5p separated by 1ds each, 8ds, close. *Leave no thread. Make another ring of 8ds, join to last p of last ring, 1ds, 4p separated by 1ds each, 8ds, close.** Repeat from * once. Tie tightly at base of 3 rings and cut.

CONSTRUCTION: Hem collar (ribbon) ends so that collar overlap is ¾″. Sew Velcro fastener to overlap on inside. Appliqué trimming over grosgrain ribbon with center decoration on outside of overlap. Sew bead at base of 3 center rings.

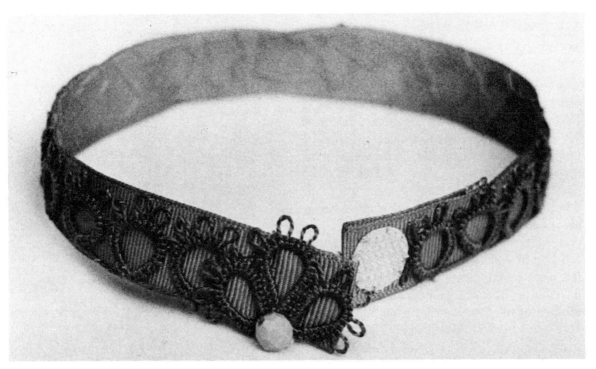

Fancy Dan dog collar

Fancy Dan dog collar with young lady

Fancy Dan dog collar

BABY BONNET

MATERIALS: Less than 1 oz. 3-ply baby wool.

Back: (Double Running Ring pattern)
(Row 1). *Ring of 5ds, p, 5ds, p, 5ds, p, 5ds,
close.** At base of first ring repeat from *.
Leave ½" yarn. *Ring of 5ds, join to last p of
1st ring, 5ds, p, 5ds, p, 5ds, close. At base of
last ring make ring of 5ds, join to last p of
next-to-last ring made, 5ds, p, 5ds, p, 5ds,
close. Leave ½" of yarn.** Repeat from * 6
times until you have 2 rows of rings, base to
base, 8 rings in length. Tie and cut. Repeat directions for back just given twice more joining
center p on right side of row just completed to
left side, center picots, of new row. Tie ball
and shuttle threads together. Join to center p
of 1st ring of row 1. *Chain of 5ds, p, 5ds.
Join to next p.** Repeat from * 20 times ending in center p of 2nd ring row 3. Tie and cut.

Sides: Repeat directions for row 1 of back
until you have a double row of rings, 22 rings
long (44-ring total). Tie and cut. Repeat directions for row 1, joining left side of row 2 to
right side row 1 by center p. Tie ball and shuttle threads together. Ring of 5ds, p, 5ds, join
to center p 2nd ring of last row, 5ds, p, 5ds,
close. *RW. Chain of 5ds, p, 5ds. RW. Ring
of 5ds, join to last p of last ring, 5ds, join to
center p of next ring (4th ring of row 2), 5ds,
p, 5ds, close.** Repeat from * along row 2.
Tie and cut.

Join Bonnet Back to Sides: Tie ball and
shuttle threads together. Join to center of
1st ring of row 1 outer edge. Make chain of
5ds, join to last p of last chain of back, 5ds,
join to center p of next ring on side (3rd ring
of row 1). *Chain of 5ds, join to next p of
back (next to last chain), 5ds, join to next p
of side (center p of 5th ring).** Repeat from
* 19 times until sides are joined to back. Tie
and cut. Finish by sewing ribbon ties on lower
front corners.

Baby bonnet

BEADED HEMP NECKLACE

MATERIALS: Soft macramé hemp or heavy rug yarn. Thirty-nine large-centered beads to contrast. (See color pages.)

Round 1: Tie ball and shuttle threads together. Ring of 2ds, 3p separated by 2ds each, 2ds, close. *RW. Chain of 2ds, p, 1ds. RW. Ring of 2ds, join to last p of last ring, 2ds, p, 2ds, p, 2ds, close.** Repeat from * 9 times. *RW. Chain of 2ds, add bead, 2ds. RW. Ring of 2ds, join to last p of last ring, 2ds, add bead, 2ds, p, 2ds, close.** Repeat from * 7 times. *RW. Chain of 2ds, p, 2ds, p, 2ds. RW. Ring of 2ds, join to last p of last ring, 2ds, add bead, 2ds, p, 2ds, close.** Repeat from * 2 more times. *RW. Chain of 2ds, add bead, 2ds. RW. Ring of 2ds, join to last p of last ring, 2ds, add bead, 2ds, p, 2ds, close.** Repeat from * 6 times, joining last ring to 1st p of 1st ring. RW. Chain of 2ds, add bead, 2ds. Tie at base of 1st ring and cut.

Round 2: Tie ball and shuttle threads together. Join to 1st p of 1st chain with 2p. *Chain of 3ds, add bead, 3ds, join to next p.** Repeat from * 4 times ending in last p of last chain with 2p. Tie and cut.

Beaded hemp necklace

WINDOW VALANCE

MATERIALS: One ball macramé twine, medium or heavy. Unbleached muslin for valance.

Tie ball and shuttle threads together. *Ring of 2ds, p, 1ds, p, 1ds, p, 1ds, p, 1ds, p, 2ds, close. RW. Chain of 2ds, 5p separated by 1ds each, 2ds, join to middle p of ring. RW.** Repeat from * for width of valance.

Window valance

FIRST PLACE MATS

(They get that name because they are so quick and easy to make they come in first in any tatting race.)

MATERIALS: Macramé hemp or heavy rug yarn (1 skein per mat).

Round 1: Tie ball and shuttle threads together. Ring of 2ds, 3p separated by 1ds each, 2ds, close. *RW. Chain of 4ds, p, 4ds. RW. Ring of 2ds, join to last p of last ring, 2ds, p, 2ds, p, 2ds, close.** Repeat from * 3 times. RW. Chain of 4ds, p, 4ds, join to last p of last ring. Chain of 4ds, p, 8ds, p, 4ds. RW. Ring of 2ds, join at bottom of chain just made between 9th and 10th ds, 2ds, join to center p of ring opposite (last ring made), 2ds, p, 2ds, p, close. RW. *Chain of 4ds, p, 4ds. RW. Ring of 2ds, join to last p of last ring, 2ds, join to center p of ring directly opposite (4th ring from beginning), 2ds, p, 2ds, close. RW.** Repeat from * 3 times. Chain of 4ds, p, 4ds, join to last p of last ring. Chain of 4ds, p, 4ds, join to 1st p of 1st ring. Chain of 4ds, p, 4ds, join to base of 1st ring. Tie and cut.

Round 2: Tie ball and shuttle threads together and join to p of 1st chain. *Chain of 3ds, p, 3ds. Join to next p.** Repeat from * around round 1. Tie and cut.

Round 3: Tie ball and shuttle threads together. Join to p of 1st chain round 2. *Chain of 4ds, p, 4ds, join to next p.** Repeat from * around round 2. Tie and cut.

Round 4: Tie ball and shuttle threads together and join to p of 1st chain of round 3. *Chain of 4ds, p, 4ds, join to next p.** Repeat from * around round 3. Tie and cut.

Round 5: Tie ball and shuttle threads together and join to p of 1st chain of round 4. *Chain of 5ds, p, 5ds, join to next p.** Repeat from * around round 4. Tie and cut.

Round 6: Tie ball and shuttle threads together and join to p of 1st chain of round 5. *Chain of 6ds, p, 6ds, join to next p.** Repeat from * around round 5. Tie and cut.

FIRST PLACE COASTER

(To match First Place Mat)

MATERIALS: Macramé hemp or heavy rug yarn.

Tie ball and shuttle threads together. Ring of 2ds, 3p separated by 1ds each, 2ds, close. RW. Chain of 4ds, p, 4ds. RW. Ring of 2ds, join to last p of last ring, 2ds, p, 2ds, p, 2ds, close. RW. Chain of 4ds, p, 4ds, join to last p of last ring. Chain of 4ds, p, 8ds, p, 4ds. RW. Ring of 2ds, join to bottom of chain just made between 9th and 10th ds, 2ds, join to center p of ring opposite (ring just made), 2ds, p, 2ds, close. RW. Chain of 4ds, p, 4ds. RW. Ring of 2ds, join to last p of last ring, 2ds, join to center p of 1st ring, 2ds, p, 2ds, close. RW. Chain of 4ds, p, 4ds, join to last p. Chain of 4ds, p, 4ds, join to 1st p of 1st ring. Chain of 4ds, p, 4ds, join to base of 1st ring. Tie and cut.

First place mats

First place coaster

BEADED CAFE CURTAIN
(30 inches wide)

MATERIALS: One skein of light (fish net) twine. Twenty large-centered beads.

Row 1: *Make ring of 3ds, 3p separated by 3ds, 3ds, close. Leave 4″ of twine.** Repeat from * until you have 21 rings. Leave 7″ of twine.

Row 2: *Make ring of 3ds, 3p separated by 3ds, 3ds, close. Leave 1¾″ of twine and join to middle picot of last ring 1st row. Leave 1¾″ of twine. Ring of 3ds, 3p separated by 3ds, 3ds, close. Leave 1¾″ of twine. Join in middle p of next-to-last ring of 1st row. Leave 1¾″ of twine.** Repeat from * across row. After you have joined to the middle p of 1st ring of 1st row, leave 1¾″ of twine. Make ring of 3ds, 3p separated by 3ds, 3ds, close. Leave 7″ of twine and join to base of 1st ring. Tie and cut.

Row 3: Tie shuttle string to middle p last ring of row 2. *Leave 1¾″ of string. Make ring of 3ds, 3p separated by 3ds, 3ds, close. Leave 1¾″ of twine. Join to middle p of next-to-last ring of row 2.** Repeat from * across row ending by tying 1¾″ of twine to middle p 21st ring of row 2.

Row 4: Tie shuttle twine in middle p of 1st ring of row 2. Leave 3½″ of twine. *Make ring of 3ds, 3p separated by 3ds, 3ds, close. Leave 1¾″ of twine. Tie in middle p of last ring of row 3.** Repeat from * across row.

Additional Length: Repeat rows 3 and 4 for the desired length of curtain. (Average will be about 9 rows, total.)

Final Row: Work according to directions for row 4 except in the middle p of each ring pull a loop of shuttle thread through center of a large bead (use a crocket hook), then pass shuttle through loop and continue working as if you had joined work to another picot.

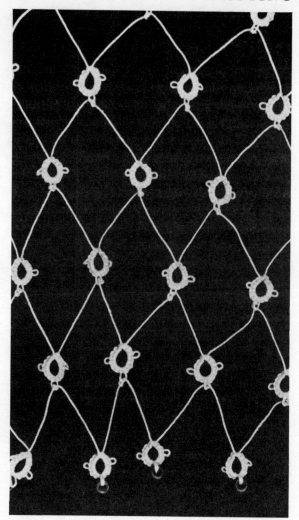

Beaded cafe curtain (detail)

FREE-FORM RUG

MATERIALS: Four skeins of rug yarn. Felt base of contrasting color (1 yard). Two skeins embroidery floss the color of rug yarn. Using this amount of yarn, rug will be approximately 4' in diameter. (See color pages.)

This rug is called free form because it is made with no specific pattern. Worked at your whim. It requires less concentration than most pieces and goes very quickly. Tie ball and shuttle threads together. Make ring of 4ds, p, 4ds, p, 2ds, close. RW. Chain of 2ds, p, 5ds, p, 1ds, join to 1st p on ring, 2ds, p, 6ds, p, 1ds, join to last p on ring, 2ds, p, 6ds, join to 1st p on 1st chain. Continue to work chains round and round center, making picots every 5 or 6ds in no set pattern . . . just as suits your eye, joining chains to picots as they turn up. When you have reached the desired rug size, fasten chain to last p, tie and cut. Using rug as pattern, cut felt underlay about ¼" overall bigger than rug. Bind edge with blanket stitch and sew rug to felt.

Free-form rug

SEA WAVE TABLETOP
(40″ × 54″ oblong)

MATERIALS: Macramé hemp or heavy rug yarn. Three large balls of a neutral color and 1 of contrast.

Round 1: Neutral. Tie ball and shuttle threads together. Ring of 4ds, p, 4ds, p, 4ds, p, 4ds, close. RW. Chain of 4ds, p, 4ds, p, 4ds. RW. Ring of 4ds, join to last p of first ring, 4ds, p, 4ds, close. RW. Chain of 4ds, p, 4ds, p, 4ds, p, 4ds. RW. Ring of 4ds, p, 4ds, join to center p, 2nd ring, 4ds, p, 4ds, close. At the base of last ring *make ring of 4ds, p, 4ds, p, 4ds, p, 4ds, close. RW. Chain of 4ds, p, 4ds, p, 4ds, p, 4ds. RW. Ring of 4ds, p, 4ds, join to center p 4th ring, 4ds, p, 4ds, close.** Repeat from * 4 times. RW. Chain of 4ds, p, 4ds, p, 4ds. RW. Ring of 4ds, join to last p of last ring, 4ds, p, 4ds, p, 4ds, close. RW. Chain of 4ds, p, 4ds, p, 4ds, p, 4ds. RW. Ring of 4ds, p, 4ds, join to center p of last ring, 4ds, join to last p of ring directly oppo-site (3rd ring back), 4ds, close. At the base of last ring *make ring of 4ds, join to last p of ring directly opposite (5th ring back), 4ds, p, 4ds, p, 4ds, close. RW. Chain of 4ds, p, 4ds, p, 4ds, p, 4ds. RW. Ring of 4ds, p, 4ds, join to center p of last ring, 4ds, join to last picot of ring directly opposite (7th ring back), 4ds, close.** Repeat from * 3 times. At the base of the last ring make ring of 4ds, p, 4ds, join to center p of first ring, 4ds, join to last p of ring directly opposite (3rd ring from the beginning), 4ds, close. RW. Chain of 4ds, p, 4ds, p, 4ds, p, 4ds, join to base of first ring, cut and tie.

Round 2: Neutral. Tie ball and shuttle threads together. Join to 2nd p of first chain round 1. Chain of 5ds, p, 5ds, p, 5ds, join to 1st p 2nd chain of 1st round (top of oblong). *Chain of 4ds, p, 4ds, p, 4ds, join to 3rd p 2nd chain of 1st round. Chain of 4ds, p, 4ds, join to 1st p 3rd chain 1st round.** Repeat from * 4 times. Chain of 4ds, p, 4ds, p, 4ds, join to 3rd p of 7th chain of 1st round. Chain of 5ds, p, 5ds, p, 5ds, join to 1st p 8th chain

Sea Wave tabletop

of 1st round (bottom of oblong). Cut and tie. Repeat above directions for corresponding side of oblong.

Round 3: Neutral. Tie ball and shuttle threads together. Join to 2nd p of 1st chain round 2. Chain of 4ds, p, 4ds, p, 4ds, p, 4ds, join to 2nd p 2nd chain round 2. Chain of 4ds, p, 4ds, p, 4ds, join to 1st p 4th chain round 2. Chain of 4ds, p, 4ds, join to 2nd p 4th chain round 2. Chain 4ds, p, 4ds, p, 4ds, join to 1st p 6th chain round 2. Chain of 4ds, p, 4ds, join to next p round 2. Chain of 4ds, p, 4ds, p, 4ds, join to first p 8th chain of round 2. Chain of 4ds, p, 4ds, join to next p round 2. Chain 4ds, p, 4ds, p, 4ds, join to 1st p 10th chain round 2. Chain of 4ds, p, 4ds, join to next p round 2. Chain of 4ds, p, 4ds, p, 4ds, join to 1st p 12th chain round 2. Chain of 4ds, p, 4ds, p, 4ds, p, 4ds, join to 1st p 13th chain of round 2 (bottom of oblong). Cut and tie. Repeat above directions for corresponding side of oblong.

Round 4: Neutral. Tie ball and shuttle threads together. Join to 2nd p first chain round 3. Chain of 4ds, p, 4ds, p, 4ds, join to 1st p 2nd chain round 3. Chain of 4ds, p, 4ds, join to next p round 3. Chain of 4ds, p, 4ds, p, 4ds, join to 1st p 4th chain round 3. Chain of 4ds, p, 4ds, join to next p round 3. Chain of 4ds, p, 4ds, p, 4ds, join to 1st p 6th chain round 3. Chain of 4ds, p, 4ds, join to next p round 3. Chain of 4ds, p, 4ds, p, 4ds, join to 1st p chain 8 round 3. Chain of 4ds, p, 4ds, join to next p round 3. Chain of 4ds, p, 4ds, p, 4ds, join to 1st p chain 10 round 3. Chain of 4ds, p, 4ds, p, 4ds, join to next p round 3. Chain of 4ds, p, 4ds, p, 4ds join to 1st p 11th chain round 3. Cut and tie. Repeat above directions for corresponding side of oblong.

Round 5: Neutral. Join ball and shuttle threads together. Join to 2nd p of 1st chain of round 4. *Chain of 4ds, p, 4ds, p, 4ds, join to 1st p of 3rd chain round 4. Chain of 4ds, p, 4ds, join to 2nd p of 3rd chain of round 4.** Repeat from * every other chain of round 4 stopping at 1st p of 11th chain. Cut and tie. Repeat above directions for corresponding side of oblong.

Round 6: Neutral. Tie ball and shuttle threads together. Join to 1st p of 1st chain of round 2. Chain of 4ds, p, 4ds, p, 4ds, join to 1st p of 1st chain of round 3. Chain of 4ds, p, 4ds, p, 4ds, join to 1st p of 1st chain of round 4. *Chain of 4ds, p, 4ds, p, 4ds, join to 1st p of 1st chain of round 5. Chain of 4ds, p, 4ds, join to next p of round 5.** Repeat from * every other chain of round 5 through chain 9. Chain of 4ds, p, 4ds, p, 4ds, join to last p of last chain of round 4. Chain of 4ds, p, 4ds, p, 4ds. Join to last p of last chain of round 3. Chain of 4ds, p, 4ds, p, 4ds, join to last p of 13th chain round 2 (last chain right side). Chain of 5ds, p, 5ds, p, 5ds, join to next p on left side round 2. Repeat above directions for corresponding side of oblong.

Round 7: Neutral. Tie ball and shuttle threads together. Join to 1st p of 1st chain of round 6. Chain of 4ds, p, 4ds, join to next p of round 6. Chain of 4ds, p, 4ds, join to 1st p, 2nd chain of round 6. Chain of 4ds, p, 4ds, join to next p of round 6. Chain of 4ds, p, 4ds, join to 1st p 3rd chain of round 6. *Chain of 4ds, p, 4ds, join to next p of round 6. Chain of 4ds, p, 4ds, p, 4ds, join to 1st p of 5th chain of round 6.** Repeat from * joining to every other chain on round 6 for 4 times. Chain of 4ds, p, 4ds, join to next p round 6. Chain of 4ds, p, 4ds, join to 1st p 14th chain of round 6. *Chain of 4ds, p, 4ds, join to next p of round 6.** Repeat from * 10 times. *Chain of 4ds, p, 4ds, p, 4ds, join to 1st p of 21st chain of round 6. Chain of 4ds, p, 4ds, join to next p of round 6.** Repeat from * every other chain of round 6 for 4 times. *Chain of 4ds, p, 4ds, join to next p of round 6.** Repeat from * 6 times to complete round. Cut and tie.

Round 8: Neutral. Tie ball and shuttle threads together. Join to p of 37th chain of round 7 (top of oblong). *Chain of 4ds, p, 4ds, p, 4ds, join to p of 39th chain of round 7.** Repeat from * every other chain of round 7 for 5 times. Cut and tie. Repeat above directions for bottom of oblong, beginning by tying ball and shuttle thread to p of 15th chain of round 7.

Round 9: Neutral. Tie ball and shuttle threads together. Join to 2nd p of 3rd chain of round 8 (top of oblong). Chain of 4ds, p, 4ds, p, 4ds, join to 1st p, 4th chain of round 8. *Chain of 4ds, p, 4ds, join to next p round 8. Chain of 4ds, p, 4ds, p, 4ds, join to next p round 8.** Repeat from * to last p of round 8 (top of oblong). Chain of 4ds, p, 4ds, p, 4ds, join to 1st p 6th chain of round 7. *Chain of 4ds, p, 4ds, join to next p of round 7. Chain of 4ds, p, 4ds, p, 4ds, join to 1st p of 8th chain of round 7.** Repeat from * every other chain around round 7 for 4 times ending last chain in 1st p of 1st chain of round 8 (bottom of oblong). *Chain of 4ds, p, 4ds, join to next p of round 8. Chain of 4ds, p, 4ds, p, 4ds, join to next p of round 8.** Repeat from * 4 times. Chain of 4ds, p, 4ds, join to last p last chain round 8 (bottom of oblong). Chain of 4ds, p, 4ds, p, 4ds, join to 1st p 28th chain of round 7. *Chain of 4ds, p, 4ds, join to next p of round 7. Chain of 4ds, p, 4ds, p, 4ds, join to 1st p 30th chain round 7.** Repeat from * every other chain on round 7 for 4 times ending last chain in 1st p 1st chain of round 8. *Chain of 4ds, p, 4ds, join to next p round 8. Chain of 4ds, p, 4ds, p, 4ds, join to next p round 8.** Repeat from * once. Chain of 4ds, p, 4ds, join to 2nd p 3rd chain of round 8 (top). Cut and tie.

Round 10: Neutral. Tie ball and shuttle threads together. Join to 1st p 1st chain round 9. *Chain of 4ds, p, 4ds, join to next p. Chain of 4ds, p, 4ds, p, 4ds, join to 1st p of chain after next (chain 3) round 9.** Repeat from * around oblong.

Round 11: Neutral. Tie ball and shuttle threads together. Join to p of 41st chain round 10 (top of oblong). *Chain of 4ds, p, 4ds, join to next p.** Repeat from * 11 times ending in p of 5th chain of round 10. Cut and tie. Tie ball and shuttle thread together. Join to p of 19th chain of round 10 (bottom of oblong). *Chain of 4ds, p, 4ds, join to next p.** Repeat from * 11 times ending in p of 27th chain round 10. Cut and tie.

Round 12: Neutral. Tie ball and shuttle threads together. Join to p of 6th chain round 11 (top of oblong). *Chain of 4ds, p, 4ds, join to next p round 11.** Repeat from * 5 times. *Chain of 4ds, p, 4ds, p, 4ds, join to 1st p 6th chain round 10. Chain of 4ds, p, 4ds, join to next p round 10.** Repeat from * every other chain round 10 for 6 times ending in last p chain 18 round 10. Chain of 4ds, p, 4ds, p, 4ds, join to 1st p round 11 (bottom of oblong). *Chain of 4ds, p, 4ds, join to next p.** Repeat from * 10 times across bottom of oblong. Chain of 4ds, p, 4ds, p, 4ds, join to 1st p 28th chain round 10. *Chain of 4ds, p, 4ds, join to next p round 10. Chain of 4ds, p, 4ds, p, 4ds, join to chain after next round 10.** Repeat from * 5 times across row 10. Chain of 4ds, p, 4ds, join to last p of 40th chain round 10. Chain of 4ds, p, 4ds, p, 4ds, join to p of 1st chain round 11. *Chain of 4ds, p, 4ds, join to next p round 11.** Repeat from * to beginning of round 12 ending in p of 6th chain round 11.

Round 13: Neutral. Tie ball and shuttle threads together. Join to p of 6th chain round 12. Chain of 4ds, p, 4ds, join to next p round 12. *Chain of 4ds, p, 4ds, join to next p, 7th chain of round 12. Chain of 4ds, p, 4ds, p, 4ds, join to 1st p of chain after next (9th chain) of round 12.** Repeat from * 6 times ending in 2nd p of 21st chain of round 12. Chain of 4ds, p, 4ds, join to next p. Chain of 4ds, p, 4ds, join to p of 22nd chain round 12. Cut and tie.

Repeat above directions for corresponding side beginning in 32nd chain round 12.

Round 14: Contrast. Tie ball and shuttle threads together. Join to p of 1st chain round 12. *Chain of 4ds, p, 4ds, join to next p of round 12.** Repeat from * 3 times. Chain of 4ds, p, 4ds, p, 4ds, join to p 1st chain round 13. *Chain of 4ds, p, 4ds, join to next p round 13.** Repeat from * 22 times. Chain of 4ds, p, 4ds, p, 4ds, join to p of 23rd chain round 12. *Chain of 4ds, p, 4ds, join to next p round 12.** Repeat from * 7 times. Chain of 4ds, p, 4ds, p, 4ds, join to 1st p 1st chain round 13 (2nd side). *Chain of 4ds, p, 4ds, join to next p round 13 second side.** Repeat from * 22 times along 13th round. Chain of 4ds, p, 4ds, p, 4ds, join to 49th chain of 12th round. *Chain of 4ds, p, 4ds, join to next p 12th round.** Repeat from * 3 times ending in 1st p 1st chain 12th round. Cut and tie.

Round 15: Contrast. Tie ball and shuttle threads together. Join to p of 1st chain 14th round. *Chain of 4ds, p, 4ds, join to next p 14th round.** Repeat from * around oblong.

Round 16: Contrast. Tie ball and shuttle threads together. Join to p of 1st chain round 15. *Chain of 4ds, p, 4ds, join to next p of round 15.** Repeat from * around oblong. Cut and tie.

Round 17: Neutral. Tie ball and shuttle threads together. Join to p of 1st chain of round 16. *Chain of 5ds, p, 5ds, join to next p round 16.** Repeat from * around oblong. Cut and tie.

Round 18: Neutral. Tie ball and shuttle threads together. Join to p of 1st chain round 17. *Chain of 5ds, p, 5ds, join to next p round 17.** Repeat from * around oblong. Cut and tie.

V

New Fashions

WOOL FRIEZE

MATERIALS: Basic wool dress. Skein of soft wool of medium weight.

Tie ball and shuttle threads together. Ring of 5ds, 5p separated by 1ds each, 5ds, p, 5ds, close. RW. Chain of 5ds, 5p separated by 5ds each, 5ds, join to 2nd p of ring. *RW. Chain of 5ds, 5p separated by 5ds each, 5ds, join to 4th p of last chain. RW.** Repeat from * for desired length.

CONSTRUCTION: Sew outer edges of trim about 3″ from skirt hem. Cut dress fabric down center of tatted strip from inside and turn back and hem so work is open. Cuff may be trimmed without cutout work.

Wool frieze

Wool frieze (detail)—white on white

TWINY SLEEVE INSET

MATERIALS: Grapefruit-sized ball of wrapping twine. Bell-sleeved top of the same or coordinating color.

Work ring of 5ds, 2p separated by 5ds, 5ds, close. RW. Chain of 2ds, p, 2ds. Ring of 5ds, 2p separated by 5ds, 5ds, close. RW. *Chain of 5ds. Ring of 4ds, join to last p of neighboring ring, 4ds, p, 4ds, p, 4ds, close. RW. Chain of 2ds, p, 2ds. Ring of 4ds, join to last p of neighboring ring, 4ds, p, 4ds, p, 4ds. RW. Chain of 5ds. Ring of 5ds, join to last p of neighboring ring, 5ds, p, 5ds, p, 5ds, close. RW. Chain of 2ds, p, 2ds. Ring of 5ds, join to last p of neighboring ring, 5ds, p, 5ds, p, 5ds, close.** Repeat from * around sleeve.

Inset and sew.

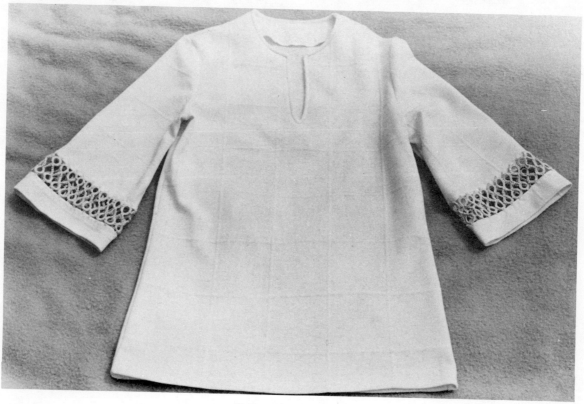

Twiny sleeve inset

MEXICAN SLEEVE TRIM

MATERIALS: Two skeins heavy rug yarn. One blouse that needs sleeves extended.

Round 1: Tie ball and shuttle threads together. Ring of 3ds, 3p separated by 3ds each, 3ds, close (top). RW. Chain of 5ds. RW. Ring of 3ds, 3p separated by 3ds each, 3ds, close (bottom). *RW. Chain of 5ds. RW. Ring of 3ds, join to last p of last ring made at top, 3ds, p, 3ds, p, 3ds, close. RW. Chain of 5ds. RW. Ring of 3ds, join to last p last ring made at bottom, 3ds, p, 3ds, p, 3ds, close. **Repeat from * around sleeve joining last p of last ring to 1st p of 1st ring. Tie and cut.

Round 2: Tie ball and shuttle threads together. Join to a center p of a ring of bottom of round 1. *Chain of 5ds, p, 5ds, join to next p at bottom of round 1.** Repeat from * around bottom of round 1. Tie and cut.

CONSTRUCTION: Stitch top of rings of round 1 to sleeve bottom.

Mexican sleeve trim

BULKY TRIM FOR ROBE

MATERIALS: Six ounces of bulky yarn (Berella by Bernat) in contrasting color to a simple robe with plain neck. (See color pages.)

Row 1: Tie ball and shuttle threads together. Make ring of 4ds, 3p separated by 4ds, 4ds, close. RW. *Chain of 4ds, p, 4ds. RW. Ring of 4ds, join to last p of last ring, 4ds, p, 4ds, p, 4ds, close. RW.** Repeat from * for skirt width. Tie and cut.

Row 2: Tie ball and shuttle threads together. Ring of 4ds, p, 4ds, join to center p of 1st ring of 1st row, 4ds, p, 4ds, close. RW. *Chain of 4ds, p, 4ds. RW. Ring of 4ds, join to last p of last ring, 4ds, join to center p of next ring of row 1 (2nd ring), 4ds, p, 4ds, close. RW.** Repeat from * across row 1.

Row 3: Tie ball and shuttle threads together. Ring of 4ds, 3p separated by 4ds each, 4ds, close. RW. Chain of 4ds, join to p in 1st chain of 2nd row, 4ds. *RW. Ring of 4ds, join to last p of last ring, 4ds, p, 4ds, p, 4ds, close. **Repeat from * across row 2, joining to chain p of row 2 as they come up.

CONSTRUCTION: Stitch border to skirt bottom. Stitch single width of yarn around sleeve bottoms, front facing and neck edge, tacking every half inch to form scallops.

Bulky trim for robe

EVENING HALTER

MATERIALS: One skein of Moonlight Berger de Nord of France (pictured) or, for more informal summer casual, use a light, bright fingering or stocking yarn. Two yards dress material, 42″ wide, plus pattern for long, gathered skirt. One-fourth yard lining material for bodice. Commercial pattern for halter. Medium—Size 32–34.

Neck Strap

Round 1: Tie ball and shuttle threads together. Ring of 3ds, 3p separated by 2ds each, 3ds, close. *RW. Chain of 4ds, p, 4ds. RW. Ring of 3ds, join to last p of last ring, 2ds, p, 2ds, p, 3ds, close.** Repeat from * 29 times. *RW. Chain of 5ds, p, 5ds. RW. Ring of 3ds, join to last p of last ring, 2ds, p, 2ds, p, 3ds, close.** Repeat from * 15 times joining last p of last ring to 1st p of 1st ring. Chain of 5ds, p, 5ds, join to base of 1st ring. Tie and cut.

Round 2 (Top of bodice): Tie ball and shuttle threads together and join to base of next-to-last ring round 1. Chain of 5ds, p, 5ds, join to p of 3rd from last chain of round 1. *Chain of 5ds, p, 5ds, join to next p round 1 (4th from last chain).** Repeat from * 11 times ending in 33rd chain of round 1. Chain of 5ds, p, 5ds, join to base of 33rd ring round 1. Tie and cut.

Round 3: Tie ball and shuttle thread together and join to p of 1st chain round 2. *Chain of 5ds, p, 5ds, join to p of next chain round 2.** Repeat from * 12 times. Tie and cut.

Round 4: Tie ball and shuttle threads together and join to p of 1st chain round 3. *Chain of 5ds, p, 5ds, join to next p round 3.** Repeat from * 11 times. Tie and cut.

Round 5: Tie ball and shuttle thread together and join to p of 1st chain of round 3. Chain of 6ds, p, 6ds, join to p of 1st chain round 4. *Chain of 6ds, p, 6ds. Join to next p round 4.** Repeat from * 10 times. Chain of 6ds, p, 6ds, join to p of last chain round 3. Tie and cut.

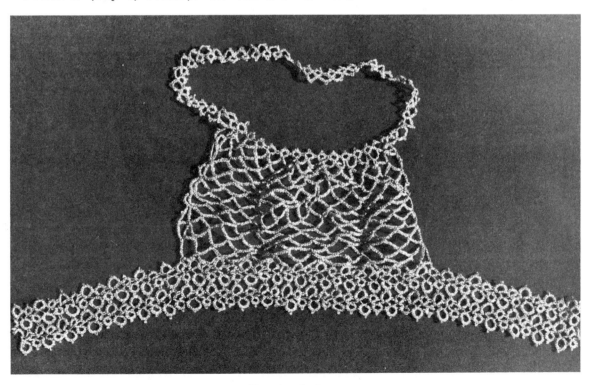

Evening halter

Round 6: Tie ball and shuttle threads together and join to p of 1st chain round 5. Chain of 6ds, join to p of 2nd chain round 5. *Chain of 6ds, p, 6ds, join to next p round 5.** Repeat from * 10 times. Chain of 6ds, join to p of last chain round 5. Tie and cut.

Round 7: Tie ball and shuttle threads together and join to p of 1st chain round 5. Chain of 7ds, p, 7ds, join to p of 1st chain round 6. *Chain of 7ds, p, 7ds, join to next p round 6.** Repeat from * 10 times ending in p of last chain round 5. Tie and cut.

Round 8: Tie ball and shuttle threads together and join to p of 1st chain round 6. Chain of 7ds, p, 7ds, join to p of 1st chain round 7. *Chain of 7ds, p, 7ds, join to next p round 7.** Repeat from * 10 times ending in p of last chain round 6. Tie and cut.

Round 9 (Bust fullness): Tie ball and shuttle threads together and join to p of 1st chain round 8. *Chain of 7ds, p, 7ds, join to next p round 8.** Repeat from * 3 times. Tie and cut. Tie ball and shuttle threads together, and join to p of 8th chain round 8. *Chain of 7ds, p, 7ds, join to next p round 8.** Repeat from * 3 times. Tie and cut.

Round 10: Tie ball and shuttle threads together and join to p of 1st chain round 8. Chain of 7ds, p, 7ds, join to p of 1st chain round 9. *Chain of 7ds, p, 7ds, join to next p round 9.** Repeat from * twice. Chain of 7ds, p, 7ds, join to p of 6th chain round 8. Chain of 7ds, p, 7ds, join to next p round 8. Chain of 7ds, p, 7ds, join to p of 4th chain round 9. *Chain of 7ds, p, 7ds, join to next p round 9.** Repeat from * 2 more times. Chain of 7ds, p, 7ds, join to last p round 8. Tie and cut.

Round 11: Tie ball and shuttle threads together and join to p of 1st chain round 10. *Chain of 7ds, p, 7ds, join to next p round 10.** Repeat from * along round 10 to last p. Tie and cut.

Round 12: Tie ball and shuttle threads together and join to 1st p round 10. Chain of 7ds, p, 7ds, join to 1st p round 11. *Chain of 7ds, p, 7ds, join to next p round 11.** Repeat from * along round 11, ending in p of last chain round 10. Tie and cut.

Round 13: Tie ball and shuttle threads together and join to p of 1st chain round 10. *Chain of 8ds, p, 8ds, join to p of 1st chain round 12.** Repeat from * along round 12, ending in p of last chain round 10. Tie and cut.

Round 14: Tie ball and shuttle threads together and join to p of 1st chain round 12. Chain of 8ds, p, 8ds, join to p of 1st chain round 13. *Chain of 8ds, p, 8ds, join to next p round 13.** Repeat from * along round 13 ending in p of last chain round 12. Tie and cut.

Round 15: Tie ball and shuttle threads together and join to p of 1st chain round 14. *Chain of 8ds, p, 8ds, join to next p round 14.** Repeat from * along round 14 to last p. Tie and cut.

Waist Band

Round 1: Ring of 3ds, 3p separated by 5ds each, 3ds, close (bottom). RW. Leave ¼" thread. Ring of 3ds, 3p separated by 3ds each, 3ds, close (top). *RW. Leave ¼" thread. Ring of 3ds, join to last p of last bottom ring, 3ds, p, 3ds, p, 3ds, close. RW. Leave ¼" thread. Ring of 3ds, join to last p of last top ring, 5ds, p, 5ds, p, 3ds, close. RW. Leave ¼" thread. Ring of 3ds, join to last p of last bottom ring, 5ds, p, 5ds, p, 3ds, close. Leave ¼" thread. Ring of 3ds, join to last p of last top ring, 3ds, p, 3ds, p, 3ds, close.** Repeat from * until you have 45 rings on bottom and 45 rings on top. Tie and cut.

Round 2: Ring of 3ds, p, 5ds, p, 5ds, p, 3ds, close (top). RW. Leave ¼" thread. Ring of 3ds, p, 5ds, join to center p of 1st top ring round 1, 5ds, p, 3ds, close (bottom). RW. Leave ¼" thread. *Ring of 3ds, join to last p of last top ring, 3ds, p, 3ds, p, 3ds, close. RW. Leave ¼" thread. Ring of 3ds, join to last p of last bottom ring, 3ds, join to center p next top ring round 1, 3ds, p, 3ds, close. RW. Leave ¼" thread. Ring of 3ds, join to last p last top ring, 5ds, p, 5ds, p, 3ds, close. RW.

*Evening halter (**photo credit: Norma Bowkett**)*

Leave ¼″ thread. Ring of 3ds, join to last p of last bottom ring, 5ds, join to p of next top ring round 1, 5ds, p, 3ds, close.** Repeat from * until you have 13 rings bottom and 13 rings top. RW. Leave ¼″ thread. Ring of 3ds, join to last p last top ring, 3ds, join top of 1st chain round 15 of bodice, 3ds, p, 3ds, close. Continue as before joining waistband to round 15 of bodice, then continue waistband beyond until you have 46 rings top and 45 rings bottom on round 2. Tie and cut.

CONSTRUCTION: Cut 2 pieces of lining material from bodice pattern. Sew darts and then sew 2 pieces together, inside out. Turn right side out and press. Cut waistband of dress fabric to correspond with width of tatted band (plus ½″ seam allowance) and your own waist measurement. Cut fabric for skirt and sew to fabric waistband. Install zipper in back with top of zipper at finished top of waistband. Stitch tatted waistband over fabric band. Sew bottom of bodice lining to inside of waistband front, then sew edges of bodice lining to tatted bodice edges.

LACE BOLERO

MATERIALS: Two skeins light stocking yarn. One-quarter yard of felt or wool for back of bolero. Any simple pattern for bolero jacket.

Top Front Left

Row 1: Ring of 5ds, 5p separated by 1ds each, 5ds, close. *Ring of 5ds, join to last p of last ring, 4p separated by 1ds each, 5ds, close.** Repeat from * 4 times (6 rings across) for shoulder top. Tie and cut.

Row 2: Tie ball and shuttle threads together. Ring of 5ds, p, 1ds, p, 1ds, join to center p of 1st ring of 1st row, 1 ds, p, 1ds, p, 5ds, close. RW. *Chain of 1ds, 5p separated by 1ds each, 1ds. RW. Ring of 5ds, join to last p of last ring, 1ds, p, 1ds, join to center p of next (2nd) ring of row 1, 1ds, p, 1ds, p, 5ds, close.** Repeat from * 4 times. Tie and cut.

Row 3: Repeat Row 2 upside down, joining center p of each chain with corresponding center p each chain of row 2.

Row 4: Ring of 5ds, 5p separated by 1ds each, 5p, close. RW. At base of 1st ring make 2nd of 5ds, p, 1ds, p, 1ds, join to center p 1st ring of row 3, 1ds, p, 1ds, p, 5ds, close. *RW. Make ring of 5ds, join to last p of last ring bottom, 1ds, 4p separated by 1ds each, 5ds, close. RW. Ring of 5ds, joint to last p of last ring top, 1ds, p, 1ds, join to center p next ring row 3, 1ds, p, 1ds, p, 5ds, close.** Repeat across row 3 so that you have 6 rings each, top and bottom. Tie and cut.

Row 5: Same as row 2, joining center p of each ring to center p bottom ring of row 4. Tie and cut.

Row 6: Same as row 3.

Row 7 (Underarm expansion): Tie ball and shuttle threads together. Ring of 5ds, 5p separated by 1ds each, 5ds, close. RW. Ring of 5ds, 5p separated by 1ds each, 5ds, close. RW. Ring of 5ds, join to last p of 1st ring row 7, 4p separated by 1ds each, 5ds, close. RW. Ring of 5ds, join to last p of top ring (2nd ring) row 7, 1ds, p, 1ds, join to center p

Lace bolero

1st ring row 6, 1ds, p, 1ds, p, 5ds, close. *RW. Ring of 5ds, join to last p last ring bottom row 7, 4p separated by 1ds each, 5ds, close. RW. Ring of 5ds, join to last p last ring top row 7, 1ds, p, 1ds, join to center p next ring row 6, 1ds, p, 1ds, p, 5ds, close. RW.** Repeat from * across row 6, ending when you have 7 rings on top and 8 rings at bottom of row 7.

Row 8 (Underarm expansion): Tie ball and shuttle threads together. Ring of 5ds, 5p separated by 1ds each, 5ds, close. *Chain of 1ds, 5p separated by 1ds each, 1ds, RW. Ring of 5ds, join to last p of last ring, 4p separated by 1ds each, 5ds, close. RW.** Repeat from * once. *RW. Chain of 1ds, 5p separated by 1ds each, 1ds. RW. Ring of 5ds, join to last p of last ring, 1ds, p, 1ds, join to center p of 1st ring row 6, 1ds, p, 1ds, p, 5ds.** Repeat from * 7 times across row 7.

Row 9: Tie ball and shuttle threads together. Ring of 5ds, 5p separated by 1ds each, 5ds. *RW. Chain of 1ds, p, 1ds, p, 1ds, join to center p of 1st chain of row 8, 1ds, p, 1ds, p,

1ds. RW. Ring of 5ds, join to last p of last ring, 4ds separated by 1ds each, 5ds, close.** Repeat from *10 times across row 8.

Row 10: Same as row 4. Repeat across row 9 ending when you have 12 rings top and 12 rings bottom.

Armhole Trim

Tie ball and shuttle threads together. Join to base of 1st ring of 1st row. *Chain of 1ds, p, 1ds, p, 1ds, p, 1ds.** Join to 1st p 1st ring of row 1. Repeat chain from * 12 times joining to: 1st p 1st ring of row 2, 1st p of 1st chain row 2, 1st p of 1st chain of row 3, 1st p of 1st ring of row 3, 1st p of 2nd ring of row 4, 1st p of 1st ring of row 4, 1st p of 1st ring of row 5, 1st p of 1st chain of row 5, 1st p of 1st chain of row 6, 1st p of 1st ring of row 6, 1st p of 2nd ring of row 7, base of 1st ring of row 7. Chain of 1ds, p, 1ds, p, 1ds, p, 1ds. RW. Ring of 5ds, join to 2nd p of 1st ring of row 7, 1ds, join to 2nd p of 4th ring of row 8, 5ds, close. RW. *Chain of 1ds, p, 1ds, p, 1ds, p, 1ds.** Join to center p of 3rd ring of row 8. Repeat from * 3 times joining to: center p of 2nd ring of row 8, center p of 1st ring of row 8, 1st p of 1st ring of row 8, base of 1st ring of row 8. Tie and cut.

Front Expansion

Tie ball and shuttle threads together. Reverse bolero. Make ring of 5ds, p, 1ds, p, 1ds, join to last p of last ring of row 10, 1ds, p, 1ds, p, 5ds, close. *RW. Chain of 1ds, 5p separated by 1ds each, 1ds. RW. Chain of 5ds, join to last p of last ring, 1ds, p, 1ds, join to last p of next-to-last ring of row 10, 1ds, p, 1ds, p, 5ds, close.** Repeat from * 5 times, joining center of rings to: last p of last ring of row 9, last p of last chain row 9, last p of last chain row 8, last p of last ring row 8, last p of last ring row 7. Chain of 1ds, 5p separated by 1ds each, 1ds, join to base of last ring of row 7. Chain of 1ds, p, 1ds, p, 1ds, p, 1ds, join to base of next-to-last ring row 7. Chain of 1ds, 5p separated by 1ds each, 1ds. RW. Ring of 5ds, p, 1ds, p, 1ds, join to last p of 2nd ring

row 7, 1ds, p, 1ds, p, 5ds, close. RW. Chain of 1ds, 5p separated by 1ds each, 1ds. RW. Ring of 5ds, join to last p of last ring, 1ds, p, 1ds, p, 1ds, join to last p of last ring row 6, 1ds, p, 1ds, p, 5ds, close. RW. Chain of 1ds, 5p separated by 1ds each, 1ds. Join to last p of last chain row 6. *Chain of 1ds, p, 1ds, p, 1ds, p, 1ds.** Join to last p last chain row 5. Repeat from * 9 times joining to: last p last ring row 5, last p next-to-last ring row 4, last p last ring row 4, last p last ring row 3, last p last chain row 3, last p last chain row 2, last p last ring row 2, last p last ring row 1, base of last ring row 1.

Front Trim

Tie ball and shuttle threads together. Join to center p of 1st chain front expansion. *Chain of 1ds, 5p separated by 1ds each, 1ds. Join to center p next chain front expansion.** Repeat from *5 times. Chain of 1ds, 5p separated by 1ds each, 1ds. Join to center p of 9th chain (3rd from last) front expansion.

Top Right Front

Make same as top left front and simply turn over when you sew to back of bolero.

Back Trim for Bottom of Bolero

Repeat pattern in row 4 of side across bolero bottom.

CONSTRUCTION: Cut bolero back. Sew shoulder and side seams, then attach bottom trim back.

LACE OVERBLOUSE

MATERIALS: Two skeins ⚹30 crochet or tatting thread. Three quarters of a yard of chiffon. Simple halter blouse pattern. Medium—size 32–34.

Center Medallion: Ring of 5 ds, 8p separated by 5ds each, close. Tie and cut. Tie ball and shuttle threads together. *Ring of 3ds, p, 3ds, p, 3ds, join to p of 1st ring, 3ds, p, 3ds, p, 3ds, close. RW. Chain of 5ds, 4p separated by 5ds each, 5ds. RW. Ring of 3ds, p, 3ds, p, 3ds, join to next p 1st ring, 3ds, p, 3ds, p, 3ds, close. RW. Chain 16ds. RW.** Repeat from * around ring. Tie and cut. Tie ball and shuttle threads together. Ring of 3ds, p, 3ds, p, 3ds, join to 1st p 1st chain last round, *4ds, p, 4ds, close. RW. Chain of 5ds, p, 5ds, RW. Ring of 4ds, join to last p of last ring, 4ds, join to next p of chain, 3ds, p, 3ds, p, 3ds, close. RW. Chain of 4ds, 4p separated by 4ds each, 4ds. RW. Ring of 3ds, p, 3ds, p, 3ds, join to next p of chain, 4ds, p, 4ds, close. RW. Chain of 5ds, p, 5ds. RW. Ring of 4ds, join to last p of last ring, 4ds, join to next p on chain, 3ds, p, 3ds, p, 3ds, close. RW. Chain of 5ds, p, 5ds, p, 5ds. RW. Ring of 3ds, p, 3ds, p, 3ds, join to 1st p of next chain with p.** Repeat from * around medallion. Tie and cut. Make 3 more medallions joining each to the last on the final round.

Round 1 (Side): Tie ball and shuttle threads together. Ring of 5ds, p, 5ds, p, 5ds, join to 4th p from bottom, side chain of bottom medallion, 5ds, p, 5ds, p, 5ds, close. RW. Chain of 5ds, 5p separated by 5ds each, 5ds, join to 4th p last ring. RW. Chain of 5ds, join to p next chain on side of bottom medallion, 8ds, join to 1st p 3rd chain on side of bottom medallion, 2ds, p, 5ds, p, 5ds, join to 4th p 1st chain. RW. Chain of 5ds, 5p separated by 5ds each, 5ds, join to 3rd p last chain. RW. Chain of 5ds, join to 2nd p 3rd chain side of bottom medallion, 8ds, join to p of 4th chain on side of bottom medallion, 2ds, p, 5ds, p, 5ds, p, 5ds, join to 4th p of last chain. RW. Chain of 5ds, 5p separated by 5ds each, 5ds, join to 4th

p last chain. RW. Chain of 8ds, join to 1st p of 5th chain on side of bottom medallion, 5ds, join to next p of 5th chain on side of bottom medallion, 2ds, p, 5ds, p, 5ds, p, 5ds, join to 4th p last chain. RW. Chain of 5ds, 5p separated by 5ds each, 5ds, join to 4th p last chain. RW. *Chain of 5ds, join to 1st p of 1st chain side of next medallion (2nd medallion from bottom), 5ds, join to next p 1st chain side of medallion, 5ds, p, 5ds, p, 5ds, p, 5ds, join to 4th p last chain. RW. Chain of 5ds, 5p separated by 5ds each, 5ds, join to 4th p last chain. RW. Chain of 5ds, join to p of 2nd chain side of medallion, 8ds, join to 1st p 3rd chain side of 2nd medallion, 2ds, p, 5ds, p, 5ds, p, 5ds, p, 5ds, join to 4th p last chain. RW. Chain of 5ds, 5p separatd by 5ds each, 5ds, join to 4th p last chain. RW. Chain of 5ds, join to 2nd p 3rd chain of medallion, 8ds, join to p of 4th chain of medallion, 2ds, p, 5ds, p, 5ds, p, 5ds, join to 4th p of last chain. RW. Chain of 5ds, 5p separated by 5ds each,

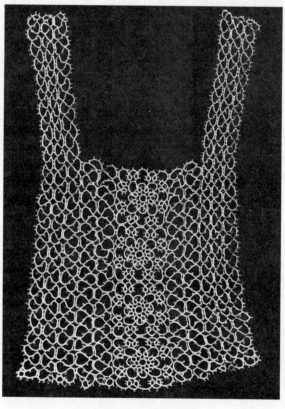

Lace overblouse

5ds, join to 4th p of last chain. RW. Chain of 5ds, join to 1st p of 5th chain of medallion, 5ds, join to 2nd p 5th chain of medallion, 5ds, p, 5ds, p, 5ds, p, 5ds, join to 4th p last chain. RW. Chain of 5ds, 5p separated by 5ds each, 5ds, join to 4th p last chain.** Repeat from * twice up side of medallions ending with chain that attaches to last 2p of last chain of last medallion, 5ds, p, 5ds, p, 5ds, p, 5ds, join to 4th p last chain. Tie and cut.

Round 2: Tie ball and shuttle threads together. Ring of 5ds, 5p separated by 5ds each, 5ds, close. RW. Chain of 5ds, p, 5ds, join to 2nd p of 1st chain round 1, 5ds, join to 2nd p 1st chain round 1, 5ds, p, 5ds, join to 2nd p 1st ring. RW. *Chain of 5ds, 5p separated by 5ds each, 5ds, join to last p last chain. RW. Chain of 5ds, join to next side p (1st p 3rd chain round 1), 5ds, join to next p (2nd p 3rd chain round 1), 5ds, join to next p (3rd p of 3rd chain round 1), 5ds, p, 5ds, p, 5ds, join to 4th p last chain.** Repeat from * along round 1 ending with chain of 5ds, join to p just above where last chain round 1 joins and was cut and tied, 5ds, p, 5ds, p, 5ds, p, 5ds, join to 4th p last chain. Tie and cut.

Round 3: Tie ball and shuttle threads together. Ring of 5ds, 5p separated by 5ds each, 5ds, close. RW. Chain of 5ds, p, 5ds, p, 5ds, p, 5ds, join to 2nd p 2nd chain round 2, 5ds, join to 3rd p 2nd chain round 2, 5ds, p, 5ds, p, 5ds, join to 1st p of ring. RW. Chain of 5ds, 5p separated by 5ds each, 5ds, join to 6th p of last chain. RW. *Chain of 5ds, join to 1st p of next chain (4th chain round 2), 5ds, join to next p of chain, 5ds, join to next p of chain, 5ds, p, 5ds, p, 5ds, join to 4th p last chain. RW. Chain of 5ds, 5p separated by 5ds each, 5ds, join to 4th p last chain. RW.** Repeat from * along round 2 and going 6" beyond top to form shoulder strap, ending with chain toward center, 5ds, p, 5ds, p, 5ds, p, 5ds. RW. Ring of 5ds, p, 5ds, join to 4th p next to last chain, 5ds, p, 5ds, p, 5ds, close. Tie and cut.

Round 4: Tie ball and shuttle threads together. Ring of 5ds, p, 5ds, join to center p 1st ring round 3, 5ds, p, 5ds, p, 5ds, close. Chain of 5ds, 5p separated by 5ds each, 5ds, join to last p of ring. RW. Chain of 5ds, p, 5ds, p, 5ds, join to 3rd p 2nd chain round 3, 5ds, join to 4th p 2nd chain round 3, 5ds, join to 5th p of 2nd chain round 3, 5ds, p, 5ds, p, 5ds, join to 1st p 1st ring. RW. Chain of 5ds, 5p separated by 5ds each, 5ds, join to 6th p 1st chain. RW. *Chain of 5ds, join to 1st p next chain (4th chain round 3), 5ds, join to next p of chain, 5ds, join to next p of chain, 5ds, p, 5ds, p, 5ds, join to 4th p of last chain. RW. Chain of 5ds, 5p separated by 5ds each, 5ds, join to 4th p of last chain. RW.** Repeat from * along round 3 ending by joining to last p of round 3, 5ds. RW. Ring of 5ds, p, 5ds, join to 4th p next to last chain, 5ds, p, 5ds, p, 5ds, close. Tie and cut.

Lace overblouse

Round 5: Tie ball and shuttle threads together. Ring of 5ds, 5p separated by 5ds each, 5ds, close. RW. Chain of 5ds, p, 5ds, p, 5ds, join to 3rd p 1st chain round 4, 5ds, join to 4th p 1st chain round 4, 5ds, join to 5th p 1st chain round 4, 5ds, p, 5ds, p, 5ds, join to 1st p of ring. RW. Chain of 5ds, 5p separated by 5ds each, 5ds, join to 6th p 1st chain. RW. *Chain of 5ds, join to 1st p next chain on side (3rd chain round 4), 5ds, join to next p, 5ds, join to next p, 5ds, p, 5ds, p, 5ds, join to 4th p last chain. RW. Chain of 5ds, 5p separated by 5ds each, 5ds, join to 4th p last chain. RW.** Repeat from * along round 4 as for round 4. Tie and cut. (Repeat rounds 1–5 for corresponding side.)

CONSTRUCTION: Cut back and 2 side pieces of chiffon from pattern. Sew back side seams. Sew tatted front to chiffon sides allowing round 5 to overlap chiffon. Sew tatted shoulder edge to chiffon shoulder edge letting tatting overlap about 1″. Hem all edges.

LACE BODICE TOP

MATERIALS: Two skeins ※30 crochet or tatting cotton. Sleeveless dress pattern with simple bodice. Medium—size 32–34. One yard ribbon for ties. (See color pages.)

Lace bodice top

Round 1 (Neck edge): Ring of 2ds, 3p separated by 1ds each, 2ds, close (top). RW. Ring of 2ds, 3p separated by 1ds each, 2ds, close (bottom). *RW. Ring of 2ds, join to last p of last ring of top, 1ds, p, 1ds, p, 2ds, close. RW. Ring of 2ds, 3p separated by 1ds each, 2ds, close.** Repeat around neck 67 times. (This gives you 69 rings top and 68 bottom.) Tie and cut.

Round 2: Ring of 2ds, 5p separated by 1ds each, 2ds, close (bottom). RW. *Ring of 2ds, p, 1ds, join to p on bottom ring (start with 1st ring) round 1, 1ds, p, 2ds, close (top). RW. Ring of 2ds, join to last p of bottom ring, 1ds, 4p separated by 1ds each, 2ds, close.** Repeat from * around round 1 until you have 68 rings top and 69 bottom. Tie and cut.

Round 3: Make cluster of * ring of 2ds, join to center p 2nd bottom ring round 2, 2ds, p, 2ds, p, 2ds, close. At base make 2nd ring of 2ds, join to center p of 3rd bottom ring round 2, 2ds, p, 2ds, p, 2ds, close. At base make 3rd ring of 2ds, 3p separated by 2ds each, 2ds, close. Tie to base of 1st ring and cut.** Repeat this cluster from * joining 1st and 2nd ring of each cluster to bottom ring round 2. It takes 34 clusters to complete round.

Round 4: *Ring of 2ds, 3p separated by 1ds each, 2ds, close (bottom). Leave ¼" thread. Ring of 2ds, p, 1ds, join to center p bottom ring of (1st) cluster round 3, 1ds, p, 2ds, close (top). Leave ¼" thread.** Repeat from * along round 3 joining to center p of center ring of each cluster. You should have 34 rings each, top and bottom. Tie and cut.

Round 5: Ring of 2ds, 7p separated by 1ds each, 2ds, close. At base of this ring make ring of 2ds, p, 1ds, join to center p 1st bottom ring round 4, 1ds, 5p separated by 1ds each, 2ds, close. Tie bases of rings together and cut. *Ring of 2ds, 3p separated by 1ds each, 1ds, join to center p of last ring, 1ds, 3p separated by 1ds each, 2ds, close. At base of this ring make 2nd ring of 2ds, p, 1ds, join to p of next ring round 4, 1ds, 5p separated by 1ds each, 2ds, close.** Repeat from * along round 4. This gives you 34 double rings.

Round 6 (Left back): *Ring of 2ds, 3p separated by 1ds each, 2ds, close (bottom). Leave ½" thread. Ring of 2ds, p, 1ds, join to 2nd p (1st) ring round 5, 1ds, p, 2ds, close (top). Leave ½" thread. Ring of 2ds, 3p separated by 1ds each, 2ds, close. Leave ½" thread. Ring of 2ds, p, 2ds, join to 6th p (2nd) ring round 5, 1ds, p, 2ds, close. Leave ½" thread.** Repeat from * along round 5 until you have 9 rings top and 10 rings bottom of this round. Tie and cut.

Round 7 (Left back): *Ring of 2ds, 3p separated by 1ds each, 2ds, close (bottom). Leave ½" thread. Ring of 2ds, p, 1ds, join to center p (1st) bottom ring round 6, 1ds, p, 2ds, close (top). Leave ½" thread.** Repeat from * along round 6 until you have 10 rings top and 11 rings bottom.

Round 8 (Left back): Repeat directions for round 5 along round 7 until you have 5 double rings and 1 single. Tie and cut.

Round 9 (Left back): Repeat directions for round 6 along round 8 until you have 10 rings top and 10 rings bottom. Tie and cut.

Round 10 (Left back): Repeat directions for round 7 along round 9 until you have 10 rings top and 11 rings bottom. Tie and cut.

Round 11 (Left back): Repeat directions for round 5 along round 10 until you have 6 double rings. Tie and cut.

Round 12 (Left back): Repeat directions for round 6 along round 11 until you have 12 rings top and 13 rings bottom. Tie and cut.

Round 13 (Left back): Repeat directions for round 7 along round 12 until you have 13 rings top and 13 rings bottom. Tie and cut.

Round 14 (Left back): Repeat directions for round 5 along round 13 until you have 7 double rings. Tie and cut.

Right Back: Make corresponding to left back beginning with 9th ring from end of 5th round.

Front: Work corresponding to left back only broaden evenly into a triangle. Use as a base ring 21 through 45 round 5.

Round 6 (Front): Should have 27 rings top and 28 rings bottom.

Lace bodice top

Round 7 (Front): Should have 28 rings top and 29 rings bottom.

. Round 8 (Front): Should have 14 double rings.

Round 9 (Front): Should have 29 rings top and 28 rings bottom.

Round 10 (Front): Should have 28 rings top and 29 rings bottom.

Round 11 (Front): Should have 14 double rings and 1 single.

Round 12 (Front): Should have 29 rings top and 29 rings bottom.

Round 13 (Front): Should have 29 rings top and 30 rings bottom.

Edge Sides: Use double-ring design of round 5.

CONSTRUCTION: Fit tatted top over chosen pattern leaving 1″ of material as underlay for lower edge of tatted bodice. Stitch tatted bodice on top of fabric. Sew ribbon ties to top neck opening in back.

EVENING PURSE

MATERIALS: One tube heavy silver thread. Velvet for purse (¼ yard). Silk cord for drawstring. Lining material (¼ yard). (See color pages.)

Tatted edging: Join ball and shuttle threads. *Ring of 3ds, 3p separated by 3ds, 3ds, close. RW. Chain of 3ds, p, 3ds. RW. Ring of 3ds, join to last p of 1st ring, 3ds, p, 3ds, p, 3ds, close. RW.** Repeat from * until long enough to edge purse from below drawstring (about 24″). Tie and cut.

Full flower: Ring of 1ds, 10p separated by 1ds each, close. Tie and cut. Join ball and shuttle threads. Join to last p of ring. *Make chain of 7ds. Join to next p.** Repeat around ring ending in last p. Tie but do not cut. Make stem from this point by working a chain of 34ds. Tie and cut. For base leaves tie ball and shuttle threads together. Chain of 2ds, 19p, 4ds (for base of stem), 12p, 1ds, tie and cut.

Half flower: Ring of 2ds, 7p separated by 2ds, 2ds, close. Tie and cut. Join ball and shuttle threads to 1st p. *Chain of 8ds, join to next p.** Repeat from * 5 times. Tie and cut. Tie ball and shuttle threads together. Make chain of 3ds, join to base of ring and tie but do not cut. Continue chain for stem with 8ds, p, 36ds, tie and cut. For base leaves tie ball and shuttle threads together. Make chain of 3ds, 25p, 2ds (or base of stem), 15p, 3ds, tie and cut.

CONSTRUCTION: Cut two pieces of velvet on purse pattern. Stitch down flowers to right side of one piece. Place two purse pieces together, right sides in. Seam sides leaving opening for drawstring. Turn inside out. Fashion lining in the same manner. Do not turn inside out. Tuck lining inside velvet purse, handstitching top edges down so raw selvage does not show. Stitch a runner for drawstring by sewing lining and purse together as indicated on pattern. Thread drawstring through purse. Hand-stitch edging around outer edge of purse.

Evening bag

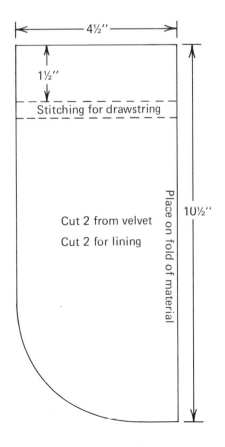

WEDDING TIARA

MATERIALS: One large ball (100 yards) of Coats and Clark's ✳1 "Speed Cro-Sheen" mercerized cotton. Glass beads or pearls optional.

Round 1: Ring of 3ds, 3p separated by 3ds each, 3ds, close. *Ring of 3ds, join to last p of last ring, 3ds, p, 3ds, p, 3ds, close.** Repeat from * until you have 20 rings joining last ring to 1st. Tie and cut.

Round 2: Tie ball and shuttle threads together. Ring of 2ds, join to center p of 1st ring round 1, 1ds, p, 1ds, p, 2ds, close. RW. Chain of 3ds, p, 3ds, p, 3ds. *RW. Ring of 2ds, join to center p of next ring round 1, 1ds, p, 1ds, join to last p of last ring, 2ds, close. RW. Chain of 2ds, p, 2ds. RW. Ring of 2ds, join to last p of next-to-last chain, 1ds, p, 1ds, p, 2ds, close. Ring of 2ds, join to last p of last ring, 1ds, 4p separated by 1ds each, 2ds, close. Ring of 2ds, join to last p of last ring, 1ds, p, 1ds, p, 2ds, close. RW. Chain of 2ds, join to p of last chain, 2ds. RW. Ring of 2ds, join to center p of next ring round 1, 1ds, p, 1ds, p, 2ds, close. RW. Chain of 3ds, join to last p of next to last ring, 3ds, p, 3ds.** Repeat from * around round 1.

Beads may be worked into design to add sparkle.

Starch heavily and block around a glass jar of slightly larger perimeter.

Wedding tiara

CLOVER COLLAR

MATERIALS: One large spool of heavy silver thread (about the size of picture-hanging wire).

Round 1: Ring of 3ds, p, 2ds, 3p separated by 1ds each, 2ds, p, 3ds. *Leave ¼" of thread. Ring of 3ds, join to last p of last ring, 2ds, 3p separated by 1ds each, 2ds, p, 3ds, close.** Repeat from * until you have 35 rings. Tie and cut.

Round 2 (Four-leaf Clover): Ring of 2ds, 7p separated by 1ds each, 2ds, close. Ring of 2ds, join to last p of last ring, 1ds, 6p separated by 1ds each, 2ds, close (outer edge). RW. Ring of 3ds, p, 2ds, p, 1ds, join to center p 1st ring round 1, 1ds, p, 2ds, p, 3ds, close. Ring of 3ds, join to last p of last ring, 2ds, p, 1ds, join to center p 2nd ring round 1, 1ds, p, 2ds, p, 3ds, close. Join to base of 2nd ring, round 2. Tie and cut.

(Triple Cluster): *Ring of 3ds, p, 2ds, p, 1ds, join to center p next ring (3rd ring) round 1, 1ds, p, 2ds, p, 3ds, close. RW. Ring of 2ds, p, 1ds, p, 1ds, join to 3rd from last p last ring outer edge, 1ds, 4p separated by 1ds each, 2ds, close. Ring of 2ds, 7p separated by 1ds each, 2ds, close. Join to base of 1st ring of this cluster. Tie and cut.

(Double Cluster): Ring of 3ds, p, 2ds, p, 1ds, join to center p of next ring round 1, 1ds, p, 2ds, p, 3ds, close. RW. Ring of 2ds, p, 1ds, join to 3rd from last p last ring of last cluster, 1ds, 5p separated by 1ds each, 2ds, close.** Repeat from * (triple cluster) two times. Then make 2 triple clusters.** Repeat from last * twice. Now add 3 double clusters which are the center of the collar. Make second half of collar to match first half, ending with four-leaf clover. Tie and cut.

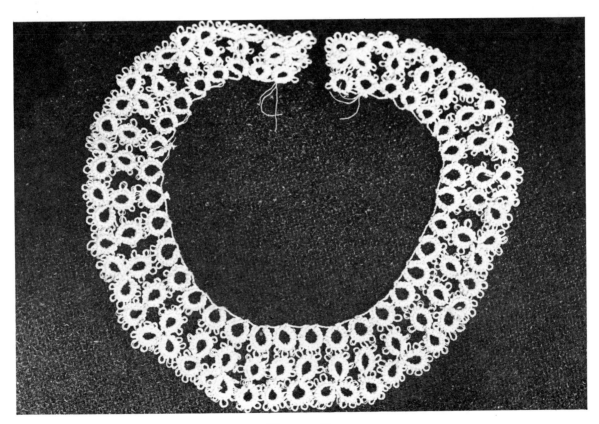

Clover collar

EXTREME COLLAR

MATERIALS: Two large balls (100 yards) of Coats and Clark's ✕1 "Speed Cro-Sheen" mercerized cotton.

Tie ball and shuttle threads together. Ring of 2ds, p, 1ds, p, 1ds, p, 2ds, close. Chain of 3ds, p, 5ds. RW. Ring of 2ds, p, 1ds, p, 1ds, p, 2ds, close. RW. Chain of 3ds, p, 4ds. RW. Ring of 3ds, 3p separated by 3ds each, 3ds, close. RW. Chain of 3ds, p, 3ds. *RW. Ring of 2ds, p, 1ds, p, 1ds, p, 2ds, close. RW. Chain of 3ds, p, 3ds. RW. Ring of 2ds, join to last p of last ring, 1ds, 4p separated by 1ds each, 2ds, close. Ring of 2ds, join to last p of last ring, 1ds, 6p separated by 1ds each, 2ds, close. Ring of 2ds, join to last p of last ring, 1ds, 4p separated by 1ds each, 2ds, close. RW. Chain of 4ds, join to p of last chain, 3ds. RW. Ring of 2ds, join to last p of last ring, 1ds, p, 1ds, p, 2ds, close. RW. Chain of 4ds, join to p of 3rd chain, 3ds. RW. Ring of 3ds, 3p separated by 3ds each, 3ds, close. RW. Chain of 5ds, join to p of 2nd chain, 3ds. RW. Ring of 2ds, p, 1ds, p, 1ds, p, 2ds, close. RW. Chain of 7ds, join to p of 1st chain, 3ds. Ring of 2ds, p, 1ds, p, 1ds, p, 2ds, close. RW. Chain of 3ds, p, 2ds. RW. Ring of 2ds, join to last p of last ring, 1ds, p, 1ds, p, 2ds, close. Chain of 3ds, p, 6ds. RW. Ring of 2ds, p, 1ds, join to center p of 3rd ring before last, 1ds, p, 2ds, close. RW. Chain of 3ds, p, 4ds. RW. Ring of 3ds, 3p separated by 3ds each, 3ds, close. Chain of 3ds, p, 3ds.** Repeat from * for desired circumference. Ten points makes an average-size collar for a woman.

Extreme collar

STRING COLLAR WITH WOODEN BEADS

Materials: Grapefruit-size ball of wrapping twine. Twenty wooden beads.

Round 1: Tie ball and shuttle threads together. Ring of 2ds, 3p separated by 2ds each, 2ds, close. *RW. Chain of 4ds, p, 4ds. RW. Ring of 2ds, join to last p of last ring, 2ds, p, 2ds, p, 2ds, close.** Repeat from * 22 times. Tie and cut.

Round 2: Tie ball and shuttle threads together and join to 1st p of 1st chain. *Chain of 4ds, p, 4ds, join to p of next chain.** Repeat from * around collar.

Round 3: Tie ball and shuttle threads together and join in 1st p of 1st chain round 1. Chain of 5ds, p, 5ds, join to p of 1st chain of round 2. *Chain of 5ds, p, 5ds, join to p of next chain round 2.** Repeat from * around round 2. Chain of 5ds, p, 5ds, join to p of last chain round 1. Tie and cut.

Round 4: Tie ball and shuttle threads together and join to p of 1st chain of round 3. Chain of 5ds, p, 5ds, join to p of next chain of round 3. *Chain of 5ds, add wooden bead, 5ds, join to p of next chain round 3.** Repeat from * around collar to next to last chain round 3. Chain of 5ds, p, 5ds, join to p of last chain round 3. Tie and cut.

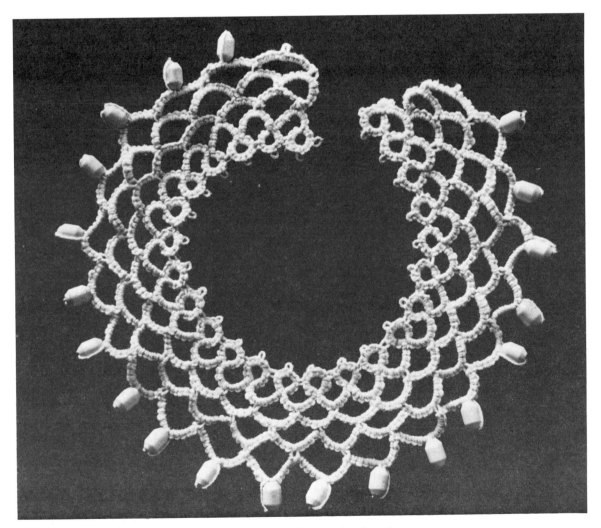

String collar with wooden beads

VI

Hang It!

BUTTERFLY AND THISTLE

MATERIALS: Two spools Dritz metallic thread for sewing machine. Two spools red buttonhole silk. Dark velvet (¼ yard). Ornate frame. Completed hanging is 8½″ ×11½″. (See color pages for full hanging.)

Butterfly Body: Work feeler in red buttonhole silk beginning with a ring of 12ds, p, 12ds, close. Tie ball thread on and make chain of 14ds, small p, 12ds, p, 12ds, join to 1st p of chain, 14ds. Ring of 12ds, p, 12ds, close. Tie and cut. Make head in red silk. Leave 2″ of thread. Make ring of 6ds, 3p separated by 6ds each, 6ds, close. Join to base p of feeler. Ring of 6ds, 3p separated by 6ds each, 6ds, close. Join tightly to base of 1st ring of head. Then, centered at the base of 2 rings, make a 3rd ring of 12ds, p, 12ds. Close and tie to beginning thread of 1st ring. Join ball thread. Chain of 14ds, join to center p of last ring, 1ds, p, 1ds, join to center p of last ring, 12ds, join to base of ring, tie and cut. For mid-section make ring of 14ds, large p, 14ds,

close. Join ball thread at base of ring. Chain of 16ds, join to center p of 1st ring, 16ds, join to base of 1st ring. Chain of 2ds, 6p separated by 2ds, 2ds, join to p of ring, 2ds, p, 2ds, join to p of ring, 2ds, 6p separated by 2ds, 2ds, join to base of ring, then join to center p at base of head. Tie and cut. For tail make ring of 14ds, p, 4ds, large p, 4ds, p, 14ds, close. Join ball thread at base of ring. Chain of 14ds, join to 1st p of tail ring. RW. Chain of 2ds, 5p separated by 2ds each, 2ds, join to base of tail. Chain of 14ds, join to last p of ring. RW. Chain of 2ds, 5p separated by 2ds each, 2ds. Join to base of work, then join tail to body.

Butterfly Wing: Work upper wing spot in red buttonhole silk beginning with ring of 2ds, 7p separated by 1ds each, close. Tie and cut. Join ball thread and make chain of 3ds, p, 3ds, join to 1st p of ring. Repeat around ring. Tie and cut. Tie gold metallic ball and shuttle threads together and join to 1st p of red spot. Make chain of 4ds, p, 4ds, join to next red p to make 1st gold scallop. Continue around red wing spot forming 8 scallops, closing in the

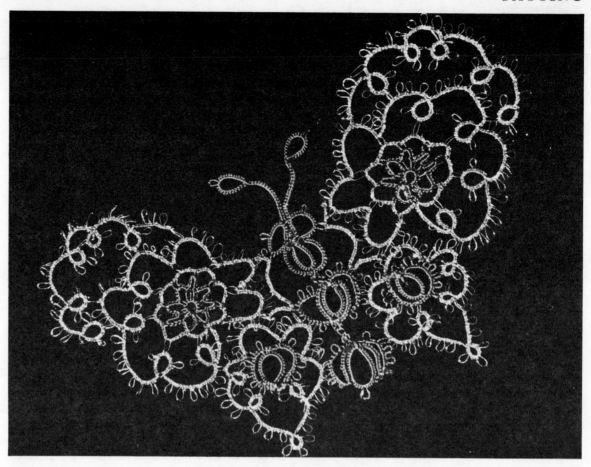

Butterfly and Thistle (detail)

same p as you started. RW. Chain of 14ds. RW. Ring of 6ds, p, 6ds, join to p of 1st gold scallop, 6ds, p, 6ds, close. RW. Chain of 3ds, 7 large p separated by 3ds each, 3ds. RW. *Ring of 6ds, p, 6ds, join to p of 2nd gold scallop, 6ds, p, 6ds, close.** Repeat from * 3 times joining end of last chain to p of 5th gold scallop. *Chain of 3ds, 7p separated by 3ds each, 3ds, join to p of 6th gold scallop.** Repeat from * joining in p of 7th and 8th gold scallops. Tie and cut. Tie ball and shuttle threads of gold together and join to 3rd p of 5th scallop. Make chain of 3ds, 3p separated by 3ds each, 3ds. RW. Ring of 6ds, p, 6ds, join to center p of 4th scallop, 6ds, p, 6ds, close. RW. Chain of 3ds, 4p separated by 3ds, 3ds. RW. Ring of 4ds, 3p separated by 4ds each, 4ds, close. RW. Chain of 3ds, 4p separated by 3ds each, 3ds. RW. Ring of 4ds, join

to last p of last ring, 4ds, p, 4ds, p, 4ds, close. RW. Chain of 3ds, 5p separated by 3ds each, 3ds. RW. Ring of 6ds, p, 6ds, join to center p of 3rd scallop, 6ds, p, 6ds, close. RW. Chain of 3ds, 4p separated by 3ds, 3ds. RW. Ring of 6ds, p, 6ds, join to 1st p of 3rd scallop, 6ds, p, 6ds, close. Tie and cut. Join upper wing to body. Tie ball and shuttle threads to center p of 6th scallop. Chain of 2ds, p, 2ds, join to bottom p of eye on head. Chain of 12ds, join to 3rd p of last scallop on body. Chain of 10ds, join to 5th p on last scallop of wing. Tie and cut.

Work bottom wing center spot in red buttonhole silk with ring of 14ds, p, 14ds, close. Join ball thread at base. Make chain of 2ds, 6p separated by 2ds each, 2ds, join to p of ring, 2ds, 6p separated by 2ds each, 2ds. Join to base of ring. Tie and cut. In gold metallic thread make ring of 3ds, p, 3ds, join to 1st p of 1st scallop of red wing spot, 3ds, p, 3ds, close. RW. Chain of 3ds, 3p separated by 3ds each, 3ds. RW. (Tail end) Ring of 3ds, 3p separated by 3ds each, 3ds, close. RW. Chain of 3ds, 3p separated by 3ds each, 3ds. RW. Ring of 3ds, p, 3ds, join to last p of 2nd scallop on red wing spot, 3ds, p, 3ds, close. RW. Chain of 3ds, 4p separated by 3ds each, 3ds, join to 5th p of last ring of body, 3ds, 3p separated by 3ds each, 3ds, join to 1st p of 2nd scallop of red wing spot. Chain of 3ds, 3p separated by 3ds each, 3ds, join to 5th p of last scallop of upper wing, 3ds, 3p separated by 3ds each, 3ds. Join to 5th p of 1st scallop of red wing spot. Chain of 3ds, p, 3ds, join to 1st p of 1st upper wing scallop, 3ds. RW. Ring of 3ds, p, 3ds, join to 3rd p of 1st wing ring, 3ds, p, 3ds, close. Chain of 3ds, 3p separated by 3ds each, 3ds, join to 1st ring of bottom wing.

Thistle Stem: With gold metallic thread make base ring of 2ds, 7 large p separated by

Butterfly and Thistle (detail)

2ds each, 2ds, close. Tie and cut. Ring of 2ds, 2p separated by 2ds each, 2ds, join to center of 1st ring, 2ds, 2p separated by 2ds each, 2ds, close. Make chain of *4ds, 1 large p (thorn), 4ds, 1 large p, 5ds, 1 large p, 6ds, 1 large p.** Repeat from * until stem is 3″ long. Tie and cut. Add 3 sets of leaves by making chain of *2ds, large p, 2ds, large p.** Repeat from * to make each set. Leaves to be approximately 3″–3½″ long. Anchor each leaf at its center at bottom of stem.

Thistle Diamond Scored Base: Join ball and shuttle threads of gold. Make chain of 1 small loop, 6ds, 4 small p separated by 6ds each, 6ds, join to top of stem, 6ds, 4 small p separated by 6ds each, 6ds, small loop, 12ds, join at beginning. Tie and cut. This will be the cup of thistle base. Arrange so that the small p are inward, with the last 12ds at the top as a base for thistledown. From the top left (as you look at thistle) make chain of 24ds and anchor in bottom p right side. From there make chain of 12ds and join to top p right side. From there make chain of 6ds and tie to right of center at the top. From top make chain of 24ds and join to bottom p on left. From bottom p left, make chain of 12ds and join to top p left. From there make chain of 6 ds and join to top just left of center. Tie and cut. Tie ball and shuttle threads together and join to 2nd from bottom p at left. Make chain of 18ds and join to top, halfway between center and right corner. From top make chain of 12ds and join to 2nd p from top on the right side. Tie and cut. Join ball and shuttle threads together and join to 2nd p from bottom on right and make chain of 18ds joining to top just left of center. From top make chain of 12ds and join to 2nd p from top on left side. Tie and cut.

ASSEMBLE PICTURE: Cut piece of velvet 2″ larger overall than backing for frame. To finish, sew thistle base and stem to velvet. Then with red buttonhole silk embroider thistle silk in loosely worked satin stitch. Silk should be approximately ¾″ long (from top of diamond-scored base). Sew butterfly to velvet. Stretch velvet over frame base and staple. Set in frame.

The Ludicrous Lion (detail)

THE LUDICROUS LION

MATERIALS: Neutral-colored burlap for base (about 1½ yards). Yellow felt (about ¼ yard). Black felt (small square). Rug yarn, 1 skein each green and orange. Heavy black embroidery floss. Two spools bright red buttonhole thread. Plywood (22″×37″) for base of picture. (See color pages for full picture.)

To obtain a pattern for the lion and the butterfly, have a photographic enlargement made of these photos. The lion measures 19½″×11½″ at its longest and highest points, and the butterfly measures 5½″ across its wing span.

Cut the body and head of lion from yellow felt; cut the tail and ruff from black felt. Stitch the lion's face in stem stitch using black embroidery floss. Edge the lion with blanket stitch using black floss. Stem stitch is used on the curve of the raised hind leg. Cut upper and lower wings of butterfly from yellow felt; cut body from black felt. Finish edge of upper wings in blanket stitch using red buttonhole silk; finish bottom wings using black embroidery floss for blanket stitch.

Tatted Ruff: In orange rug yarn make ring of 3ds, p, 3ds, p, 3ds, close. *Leave ½″ of yarn. Make second ring of 3ds, join to last p of 1st ring, 3ds, p, 3ds, p, 3ds, close.** Repeat from * until you have a circle of 13 rings, joining the first ring to the last. Tie and cut. Tie ball and shuttle threads together and join to center p of first ring. *Chain of 2ds, 4p, 2ds. Join to center p of next ring.** Repeat from * around ruff. Tie and cut. This ruff can be used as a pattern for cutting out the black-felt underlay.

The Ludicrous Lion (detail)

Lion's Tatted Tail: In orange rug yarn make ring of 3ds, p, 3ds, p, 3ds, p, 3ds, close. At the base of this ring start a second ring of 2ds, p, 1ds, p, 1ds, p, 2ds, close. Tie and cut. Tie ball and shuttle threads to 2nd p of 1st ring to make chain of 3ds, p, 1ds, join to 1st p of 1st ring, 1ds, p, 1ds, p, 2ds, join to 1st p of 2nd ring, 3ds, large p, join to center p of last ring, 3ds, join to last p of last ring, 2ds, p, 1ds, p, 1ds, join to 1st p of 1st ring, 1ds, p, 3ds. Tie to 2nd p of first ring and cut. Use tatted tail as pattern to cut black-felt underlay.

Jungle Floor: With dark green rug yarn make ring of 3ds, p, 3ds, p, 3ds, p, 3ds, close. RW. Tie on ball thread and make chain of 3ds. RW. Ring of 3ds, p, 3ds, p, 3ds, p, 3ds, close. RW. *Chain of 3ds. RW. Ring of 3ds, join to 1st p of 1st ring, 3ds, p, 3ds, p, 3ds, close.** Repeat from * until top of the design is 20 rings across. Tie and cut.

Butterfly: Using red buttonhole silk, tat edging for wings as follows: Fasten ball and shuttle threads to inner edge of upper wing (near head). *Make chain of 2ds, large p, 2ds. Join to blanket stitch edging on wing.** Repeat from * around upper wing to where it joins lower wing. At this point embroider a line in stem stitch with red buttonhole silk to separate upper wing from lower. Tat two spots for upper wing in heavy black floss making

ring of 2ds, 7p separated by 2ds each, close. Tie and cut. Sew wing spots to wings.

Butterfly Head: Tat head and feelers with black floss. Start with ring for eye of 3ds, p, 2ds, p, 2ds, p, 3ds, close. Make 2nd eye ring at the base of the 1st using the same pattern. Tie together and cut. Start end of feeler with a ring of 6ds, large p, 6ds, close. Join ball thread and make chain of 24ds, join between two eye rings, 24ds. Ring of 6ds, large p, 6ds, close. Tie and cut. Sew to top of butterfly body.

Jungle Vine: Tie ball and shuttle threads of green rug yarn. Start from top of vine. Make chain of 1ds, 2 large p, 3ds, 3 large p, 2ds, 1 medium p, 5ds, 1 large p, 4ds, 4 large p, 1ds, 2 medium p, 3ds, 4 large p, 3ds, 6 large p, 4ds, 1 medium p, 2 large p, 1 medium p, 3ds, 4 medium p, 4 large p, 3ds, 3 large p, 3ds, 6 medium p, 5 ds, 5 large p, 1ds, 4 large p, 1ds, 3 large p, 4 ds, 5 medium p, 5 ds, 3 small p, 2ds, 4 small p, 4ds. Tie and cut. Sew as pictured as a twisting jungle vine at left of lion. For smaller vine join ball and shuttle threads. From the top make a chain of 3ds, 3 medium p, 15ds, 4 medium p, 1ds, 7 large p, 1ds, 3 medium p, 12 ds, 5 medium p, 1ds, 5 medium p, 1ds, 4 large p, 8ds, 2 medium p, 1ds, 3 small p, 1ds, 2 large p, 1ds, 3 small p, 1 large p, 1 small p, 1ds, 1 small p, 3ds. Tie and cut. Sew as pictured as twisting vine.

Flowers: Out of red buttonhole silk make ring of 5ds, 6 large p, 5ds, close. Ring of 5ds, 7 large p, 5ds, close. Ring of 5ds, 7 large p, 5ds, close. Sew the 3 rings as flower on top of one vine. Repeat design for the top of 2nd vine and repeat again with slightly smaller picots for the lower part of vine to lion's right. Embroider centers of rings with black french knots.

ASSEMBLE PICTURE: Cut a piece of burlap approximately 26″×43″ (or 2″ larger overall than plywood backing). Center and sew design in place on burlap. Stretch taut and staple edges over a piece of light plywood cut 22″×37″. Cut 4 strips of light wood to frame and nail down.

GARDEN OF EDEN

MATERIALS: Felt for background, sand-colored, 20"×12". Light green felt for snake, 12"×7". Small pieces of red and yellow felt for apple and bee. Light fingering yarn in dark green, red-orange, purple, and yellow. Less than 1 skein of each color needed. Embroidery floss to match red-orange, green, yellow, and purple yarns, light green snake, and apple. Also one skein of black. (See color pages.)

Cut out snake. If you would like a pattern for the snake, have a photostatic enlargement made from the photo in the book. The snake should measure 11"×6½" at its longest and widest points. Embroider eyelashes and jaw in

Garden of Eden

stem stitch. Attach snake to background with buttonhole stitch. Outline mouth in stem stitch and put in teeth in black. Cut out apple and buttonhole stitch to background. Cut out bee and buttonhole stitch to background, head last. Embroider eyes and feelers in purple. Embroider caption in stem stitch.

Apple Stem (*dark green yarn*): Tie ball and shuttle threads together. Chain of 10ds. Knot. At base of knot make a ring of 10ds, p, 8ds, close. At base make second ring of 8ds, p, 10ds, close. Cut and tie.

Bottom Vine (*dark green yarn*): Tie ball and shuttle threads together. Chain of 34ds, pull together slightly to curve, p (at least ¼" long), 2ds, p, 1ds, p, 2ds, p, 1ds, p, 3ds, p, 2ds, p, 3ds, p, 2ds, p, 1ds, p, 1ds, p, 2ds, p, 2ds, p, 1ds, p, 3ds, p, 2ds, p, 2ds, p, 3ds, p, 2ds, p, cut and tie.

Purple Flower for Vine: Ring of 2ds, p, 6ds, p, 6ds, p, 2ds, p, 3ds, close. Ring of 3ds, join to last p of last ring, 2ds, p, 6ds, p, 6ds, p, 2ds, close. Cut and tie. Tie ball and shuttle threads together. Join to center p of 1st ring. Chain of 4ds, 7p, 6ds, join to 3rd p of 1st ring, chain of 6ds, join to last p of last chain, 4p, 6ds, join to 2nd p of 2nd ring. Chain of 6ds, join to last p of last chain, 6p, 4ds, join to center p 2nd ring. Cut and tie.

Snake Trim Back (*red-orange*): Tie ball and shuttle threads together. Ring of 2ds, p, 2ds, close. (All rings for snake's back will be 2ds, p, 2ds.) RW. Chain of 6ds. RW. Ring. RW. Chain of 7ds. RW. Ring. RW. Chain of 7ds. RW. Ring. RW. Chain of 5ds. RW. Ring. RW. Chain of 5ds. RW. Ring. RW. Chain of 7ds. RW. Ring. RW. Chain of 7ds. RW. Ring. RW. Chain of 7ds. RW. Ring. RW. Chain of 7ds. RW. Ring. RW. Chain of 6ds. RW. Ring. RW. Chain of 6ds. RW. Ring. RW. Chain of 7ds. RW. Ring. RW. Chain of 7ds. RW. Ring. RW. Chain of 7ds. RW. Ring. RW. Chain of 7ds. RW. Ring. RW. Chain of 6ds. RW. Ring. RW. Chain of 8ds. RW. Ring. RW. Chain of 8ds. RW. Ring. RW. Chain of

6ds. RW. Ring. RW. Chain of 6ds. RW. Ring. RW. Chain of 8ds. RW. Ring. RW. Chain of 7ds. RW. Ring. RW. Chain of 8ds. RW. Ring. RW. Chain of 8ds. RW. Ring. RW. Chain of 8ds. RW. Ring. RW. Chain of 9 ds. RW. Ring. RW. Chain of 8 ds. RW. Ring. RW. Chain of 8ds. RW. Ring. RW. Chain of 8 ds. RW. Ring. RW. Chain of 8ds. RW. Ring. RW. Chain of 8ds. RW. Ring. RW. Chain of 8ds, RW. Ring. RW. Chain of 9ds. RW. Ring. RW. Chain of 8ds. RW. Ring. RW. Chain of 8ds. RW. Ring. RW. Chain of 7ds. RW. Ring. RW. Chain of 9ds. Cut and tie. (Eyebrow): Tie ball and shuttle threads together. Chain of 8ds. RW. Ring. RW. Chain of 7ds. RW. Ring. RW. Chain of 7ds. RW. Ring. RW. Chain of 7ds. Cut and tie.

Rosy Cheek of Snake: Ring of 2ds, p, 2ds, p, 2ds, p, 2ds, close. *Ring of 2ds, join to last p last ring, 2ds, p, 2ds, p, 2ds, close.** Repeat from * 2 times joining last p of last ring to 1st p of 1st ring. Cut and tie.

Flower for Snake Cheek: Ring of 1ds, p, 1ds, p, 1ds, p, 1ds, p, close. Cut and tie.

Small Yellow Flowers above Snake (make 3): Ring of 1ds, p, 1ds, p, 1ds, p, 1ds, p, close. Cut and tie.

Small Red-Orange Flowers above Snake (make 3): Ring of 1ds, p, 1ds, p, 1ds, p, 1ds, p, 1ds, p, close. Cut and tie.

Purple Flower (right): Ring of 1ds, 9p of at least a ½″, close. Cut and tie.

Large Yellow Flower: Ring of 3ds, p, 3ds, p, 3ds, p, 3ds, close. *Ring of 3ds, join to last p of last ring, 3ds, p, 3ds, p, 3ds, close.** Repeat from * 3 times. Joining last p of last ring to 1st p of 1st ring. Cut and tie.

Hanging Flowers: *Ring of 1ds, p, 1ds, p, 1ds, p, 1ds, p, close. Leave ½″ of yarn.** Repeat from * making a chain of 9 purple flowers and 11 yellow.

Bee Wing (yellow): Join ball and shuttle threads together. Ring of 4ds, 9p, 4ds, close. Cut and tie. Make 2.

Rear of Bee (red-orange): Join ball and shuttle threads together. Ring of 4ds. RW. Chain of 2ds, 5p separated by 1ds each, 2ds. RW. Ring of 4ds, close. Cut and tie.

Back of Bee Head (red-orange): Tie ball and shuttle threads together. Chain of 14ds. Cut and tie.

Stitch all tatted trims and flowers to bases.

MERIT AWARDS

MATERIALS: Heavy cotton embroidery thread (perle 15 met DMC 3) in pink, blue, and wine. Three pieces of felt, 6″×12″, one each in purple, maroon, and peach. Three plywood backings 9″×4″. (These can easily be made in any size, just vary the length of the edging accordingly.)

Merit awards

Winner (Wine lace on peach)

Edging is ring of 3ds, p, 3ds, p, 3ds, p, 3ds, close. *Ring of 3ds, join to last p of 1st ring, 3ds, p, 3ds, close.** Repeat from * around base. Dot for "i" should be tatted with ring of 1ds, p, 1ds, p, 1ds, p, 1ds, p, 1ds, p, 1ds, p, 1ds, close. Tie and cut.

Sinner (Pink lace on purple)

Ring of 1ds, 7p separated by 1ds each, 1ds, close. *Ring of 1ds, join to last p of last ring, 6p separated by 1ds each, 1ds, close.** Repeat from * around base. Dot for "i" should be tatted with ring of 1ds, 7p separated by 1ds each, 1ds, close. Tie and cut.

Thinner (Blue lace on maroon)

Tat edging of ring of 3ds, p, 3ds, p, 3ds, p, 3ds, close. *Ring of 3ds, join to last p of 1st ring, 3ds, p, 3ds, p, 3ds, close.** Repeat from * around base. Dot for "i" should be tatted with ring of 7ds, p, 7ds, close. Tie and cut.

CONSTRUCTION: Using cross stitch, embroider words on felt. Staple firmly in place on plywood backing. Stitch edging in place.

HEXAGON SAMPLER

MATERIALS: Four co-ordinating shades of silk thread (✳8). One spool Dritz metallic thread for sewing machine. Satin backing of contrasting color. Completed size 8″×10″.

This sampler is made up of 3 different tatted hexagon patterns. Work each pattern 4 times, once in each color.

Ring of Rings

Round 1: *Make ring of 6ds, p, 6ds, close. Leave ¼″ thread.** Repeat from * 5 times tying 1st ring to last with ¼″ thread between them. Tie and cut.

Round 2: Ring of 3ds, 3p separated by 3ds each, 3ds, close. *Join to p of ring of round 1. At base of last ring make 2nd of 3ds, join to last p of last ring, 3ds, 2p separated by 3ds each, 3ds, close. Leave ¼″ thread. Ring of 3ds, join to last p of last ring, 3ds, 2p separated by 3ds each, 3ds, close.** Repeat from * around round 1 joining 1st ring to last. Tie and cut.

Six-point Star

Tie ball and shuttle threads together. Ring of 2ds, 3p separated by 1ds each, 2ds, close. *Ring of 2ds, join to last p of last ring, 2ds, 4p separated by 2ds each, 2ds, close. Ring of 2ds, join to last p of last ring, 1ds, p, 1ds, p, 2ds, close. RW. Chain of 12ds. RW. Ring of 2ds, join to p of last ring, 1ds, p, 1ds, p, 2ds, close.** Repeat from * 5 times ending with ring of 2ds, join to last p of last ring, 4p separated by 2ds each, 2ds, close. Ring of 2ds, join to last p of last ring, 1ds, p, 1ds, join to 1st p of 1st ring, 2ds, close. Tie and cut.

Hexagon sampler

Double Ringer

Tie ball and shuttle threads together. Ring of 3ds, 3p separated by 3ds each, 3ds, close. *Starting at the base of the last ring make a 2nd of 3ds, join to last p of last ring, 3ds, p, 3ds, p, 3ds, close. RW. Chain of 3ds, p, 3ds, close. RW. Ring of 3ds, join to last p of last ring, 3ds, p, 3ds, p, 3ds, close.** Repeat from * until you have 6 double rings and 6 joining chains. Tie and cut.

ASSEMBLE PICTURE: Attach tatted hexagons to satin in rows, alternating color patterns. Embroider double outline on satin using gold thread and chain stitch.

VII

Blocking and Care of Tatting

How to block a fine white tatted collar that got absolutely grubby when you were working on it: Swish it gently in warm, soapy water and bleach. Let soak five or ten minutes, suds a bit but be careful not to twist or wring. Rinse the same way. Lay out on a towel and blot with a second towel.

Blocking for tatting is about the same as the system used for knits. Use a towel pinned around an ironing board, a firm pillow wrapped in a towel or a good piece of cork (like a dart board) wrapped in a towel to protect the surface of the lace. (I use a pillow, and not a very firm one at that, but it comes

Blocking tatted lace

out just fine. I'd rather use a dart board because that's hard to beat for quaintness, but I don't have a dart board.)

Early books suggest dipping collar in starch. That works but I like the following method better. Lay damp collar out on towel-covered base. Shape and pin it down. (Be sure to use rust-proof pins. I prefer those with small colored plastic heads since they are easy to spot and handle.) Do not pin through stitches but peg on rings and picots with tension on the rings. I pin only the picots that want to curl up, using just enough tension to keep them straight. If too much tension is on picots, they form unattractive corners. Most picots behave themselves after blotting, anyway.

Once pinned, spray the collar with starch being careful to hold the pressurized can the prescribed 8″–10″ from the lace or the picots will block up.

Just before collar is completely dry, take out pins. At this point I find the collar will lie quite flat without them except for a few maverick loops which I repin.

When dry, remove all pins and go over collar with a flatiron. Add another spray of starch on the back side if you really want the lace stiff. Spray starches also help lace shed dirt.

YARNS AND HEMPS

Larger threads and ropes seldom need to be washed or blocked. A moderate steam iron will usually shape them as you wish. If you use wool yarn which has gotten dirty, wash with a cold-water soap, rinse thoroughly, and block damp as you would a lace collar.

PICTURES AND DECORATIONS

Wall hangings and pictures may be sprayed with clear Scotchgard to protect from dirt and dust.

STORAGE

Heavy rugs should be stored rolled up. Fine laces are best wrapped in tissue paper or clear plastic wrap over cardboard backing.

LIFE OF LACE

And how long will tatting last? That's hard to estimate. My family is still using pillow cases trimmed with tatting made by my great-grandmother at the turn of the century, and archaeologists have unearthed samples in fair shape from ancient China.

Given a steady hand and a good knot, your work should withstand the ages.

Appendixes

Abbreviations Used

ds = double stitch
ss = single stitch (step 1 of double stitch)
p   = picot
RW = reverse work

Glossary of Embroidery Stitches

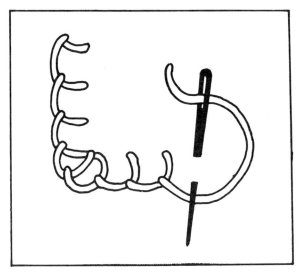

Blanket Stitch

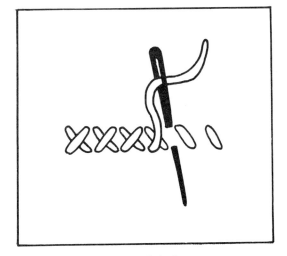

Cross Stitch

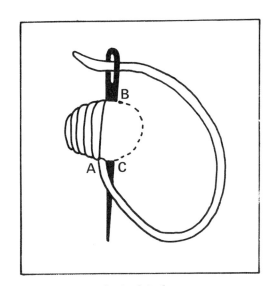

Satin Stitch

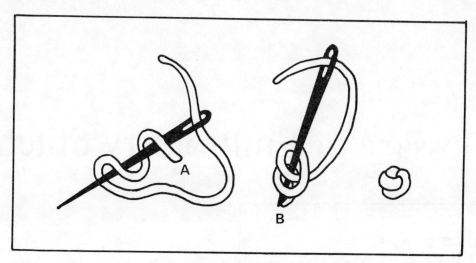

French Stitch

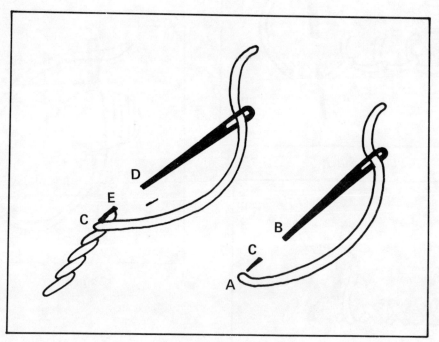

Stem Stitch

Sources of Supply and Knowledge

Local variety stores are usually the handiest sources of tatting supplies. Most still carry some brand of small shuttle with a fair selection of crochet and tatting threads and yarns, and occasionally tatting directions can be found among the "How To" booklets. Hobby and knit shops and macramé suppliers offer a wealth of ideas for creative tatters, and fanatics like myself also haunt rope warehouses and supply centers for commercial fishermen.

In large cities the Yellow Pages of the phone book make good reading under the headings of Yarn, Weaving, and Craft Supplies; and trimming shops offer the most fascinating shopping of all. There's a string of them on Sixth Avenue, New York City, stocking marvelous beads, bangles, and shimmering spools of silk and satin cords.

If you're homebound, there are catalogues in ever-increasing numbers. I've listed only a few, but knitting and needlework magazines carry advertisements for same. Another way to keep current is to subscribe to the newsletter of the International Old Lacers. The organization is usually described as "a group of sweet little old ladies," but they seem not to mind the slur and go about their business with useful efficiency. Through them you can locate tatting members all over the world—useful for those seeking tatting lessons—and ads in the newsletter feature specialty products (such as oversized shuttles) which are difficult to find elsewhere.

For serious craftsmen there is the American Crafts Council, which maintains a remarkable library of current and historical craft books along with portfolios of about 1,800 contemporary American craftsmen. In addition, the council publishes many useful booklets of its own including the *New York Guide to Craft Courses* and lists of suppliers all over the U.S.A.

USEFUL ORGANIZATIONS

American Crafts Council, 44 West 53 Street, New York, N.Y. 10019.

International Old Lacers, Mrs. Mary Cole, Membership, Rural Route 1, 23955 SW 157th Avenue, Homestead, Fla. 33030.

CRAFT BOOKS

American Crafts Guide, Gowsha, *Times Mirror,* San Jose, Calif. 1973. A comprehensive directory to craft shops, galleries, shows, schools, museums, and studios.

Craft Sources, Paul Colin and Deborah Lippman, M. Evans and Co., New York, distributed by J. B. Lippencott Co., E. Washington Square, Philadelphia, Pa. 19105.

Contemporary Crafts Market Place, American Crafts Council, 44 West 53 Street, New York, N.Y. 10019, the 1975–76 list of suppliers, courses, audio-visual sources, galleries, organizations, and publishers.

The following books are out of print but will be worth a trip to the rare book section of a large public library or museum if you are a real tatting buff:

Nichols, E. A. *A New Look in Tatting, Flowers, Leaves and Picture Composition.* Newton, Mass.: C. T. Branford Co., 1952. A highly original work on the creation of tatted pictures, quite unlike anything I've ever come across. It gave me a completely new outlook on tatting and is still sparking my imagination.

Riego de la Branchardiere, E. *The Royal Tatting Book.* London: Simpkon, Marshall and Co., 1868. Mlle. Riego de la Branchardiere cranked out dozens of handiwork books in the 1860s, which libraries have bound together as a collection. And, despite the fact that the lady called picots by the old term, "pearls," she still has valid ideas for the modern tatter.

Hoare, Katharin. *The Art of Tatting.* London: Longmans, Green & Co., 1910. Lady Hoare's classic *The Art of Tatting,* which she wrote under the patronage of the Queen of Romania, is my favorite. It is a rich book, lavishly printed; inspiring the modern tatter and thought-provoking for the modern woman.

New books (and reissued old ones) on tatting have appeared in recent years as interest in this art form grows. You may find these helpful and of interest:

Auld, Rhoda. *Tatting: The Contemporary Art of Knotting with a Shuttle.* New York: Van Nostrand-Reinhold, 1974.

Groves, Sylvia. *The History of Needlework Tools and Accessories.* New York: Arco, 1973.

Waller, Irene. *Tatting: A Contemporary Art Form.* Chicago: Henry Regenery Co., 1974.

SHUTTLES, STRING, AND YARN SUPPLIERS

Bell Yarn Company, 35 Clay Street, Brooklyn, N.Y. 11222.

Magnolia Weaving, 2635 29th Avenue W, Seattle, Wash. 98199.

School Products Co., 1201 Broadway, New York, N.Y. 10001.

Serendipity Shop, 1523 Ellenwood, Des Plaines, Ill. 60016, offers traditionally shaped shuttles in large sizes.

The Handweaver, 460 First Street East, Sonoma, Calif. 95475.

Shuttlecraft, P.O. Box 41635, Chicago, Ill. 60641 for super-sized Morgan yarn shuttle and tatting kits.

Lee Wards, Creative Crafts Center, Elgin, Ill. 60120.